Advance Praise for *The Translator's Daughter*

"I love how memoir engages with the art of looking back, of trying to understand who we were, where we truly come from, and how we got to where we are. In *The Translator's Daughter*, Grace Loh Prasad looks back with such thoughtfulness, care, and wonder. This is a searching, heartfelt memoir about family, communication, loss, and the very idea of origin stories."
—Beth Nguyen, author of *Owner of a Lonely Heart*

"*The Translator's Daughter* is a stunning tribute to the complexities of growing up as a third-culture kid, an honest and moving chronicle of the 'abundance and loss' of living across languages and continents."
—Shawna Yang Ryan, author of *Green Island*

"*The Translator's Daughter* moves from Taipei to San Francisco and back as if they were rooms of the same house, telling the story of a woman discovering her roots while simultaneously planting new ones as she creates a life on her own terms. Prasad's sharp intelligence and fierce love for her family are on every page of this beautiful book."
—Grace Talusan, author of *The Body Papers*

"You can really feel the two decades Prasad put into this memoir. This is careful, considered prose and thought from a writer to both anticipate and learn from. A marvelous debut."
—Matthew Salesses, author of *The Sense of Wonder*

"Grace Loh Prasad interrogates the distance between the homes we have and the homes we long for with the compassion and precision of one who has spent her entire life attuned to language. 'We were always half a world apart,' she writes; her essays bridge that gap in innovative ways, using family photos, mythical women, and Taiwanese films. Moving fluidly between the personal and the political, this memoir is a remarkable addition to Taiwanese American literature."

—Jami Nakamura Lin, author of *The Night Parade*

"*The Translator's Daughter* is a soulful and profound meditation on family, diaspora, and grief. How do we construct a life far away from our loved ones, and what do we lose? How do we preserve all that we have been given? Grace Loh Prasad tackles these questions with honesty and beauty, while also illuminating Taiwan's culture, history, and hard-won path to democracy. I savored this book."

—Michelle Kuo, author of *Reading with Patrick*

THE TRANSLATOR'S DAUGHTER

MACHETE
Joy Castro and Rachel Cochran, Series Editors

THE TRANSLATOR'S DAUGHTER

A Memoir

Grace Loh Prasad

MAD CREEK BOOKS, AN IMPRINT OF
THE OHIO STATE UNIVERSITY PRESS
COLUMBUS

Published by Mad Creek Books, an imprint of The Ohio State University Press.

Library of Congress Cataloging-in-Publication Data
Names: Prasad, Grace Loh, 1969– author.
Title: The translator's daughter : a memoir / Grace Loh Prasad.
Other titles: Machete.
Description: Columbus : Mad Creek Books, an imprint of The Ohio State University Press, [2024] | Series: Machete | Summary: "A memoir about navigating linguistic, cultural, political, and generational barriers as a Taiwanese American immigrant trying to build a connection with her birthplace"—Provided by publisher.
Identifiers: LCCN 2023040738 | ISBN 9780814258972 (paperback) | ISBN 0814258972 (paperback) | ISBN 9780814283288 (ebook) | ISBN 0814283284 (ebook)
Subjects: LCSH: Prasad, Grace Loh, 1969– | Prasad, Grace Loh, 1969—Family. | Taiwanese Americans—United States—Biography. | Immigrants—United States—Biography. | Taiwanese—Taiwan—Biography. | Return migration—Taiwan.
Classification: LCC E184.T35 P73 2024 | DDC 973/.049925—dc23/eng/20231012
LC record available at https://lccn.loc.gov/2023040738

Cover design by adam bohannon
Text design by Juliet Williams
Type set in Cambri

To my parents, Dr. I-Jin Loh and Dr. Lucy Tian-Hiong Loh:
Thank you for making me everything that I am and for
teaching me to love where I came from.

To my son, Devin:
Be the architect of your own story: make art, don't wait.

I am born into sound.
My mother screaming, my father comforting her
Words exchanged in a language I already know deep inside
though it will not form on my tongue for almost a year.

The sound is my home
sustaining me like an invisible organ
It is the bell ringing at the center of the universe
Until one day I am separated from it.

Half a turn on the earth's axis
Twenty hours airborne, ears popping
The nonstop hum I can't escape getting louder and louder.

Later they tell me
It was for my own good:
They traded my tongue for wings.

Contents

Author's Note

Writing a memoir over more than two decades of one's life presents many challenges. In my case, Taiwanese politics and language have evolved to such an extent that it's necessary to provide some context and explain some of my choices.

A couple of my essays describe the excitement of Taiwan's emerging democracy, including the first time ever that the opposition Democratic Progressive Party won the presidency in 2000. This was a stunning development in a country that had been a one-party dictatorship not that long ago in the past. My family and Taiwan had high hopes for Chen Shui-bian, and while he did some good things during his two terms, his career was essentially ended by a corruption scandal and prison sentence. I'm well aware that he no longer commands the respect he once did and want to clarify that my writing only addresses the optimism of his rise and not his eventual fall from grace. However, Taiwan's democracy is stronger than ever, to the point where it is now considered unremarkable and business as usual. And it bears mentioning that Taiwan has surpassed the US in terms of electing and embracing its first female president, the highly capable Tsai Ing-wen.

Language is one of the principal topics in my memoir. As the daughter of someone who was an authority on language, I am constantly humbled by how much I don't know, but also how much of language is subjective and ever-shifting. When I started writing this memoir, most English signage in and around Taipei used the Wade-Giles system of romanization to render Mandarin place names into phonetic English. It's what my parents used and what I grew up with. But Chen's successor as president, Ma Ying-jeou of the Kuomintang, pushed for the use of pinyin romanization which is more recognized across the Mandarin-speaking world, and it has become the de facto standard. I have throughout my life known the town where my parents lived as Sanhsia; the pinyin spelling "Sanxia" feels wrong to me, so in this case I am using Wade-Giles, but most other place names are romanized in pinyin.

I should also mention that anytime I reference the "Taiwanese" language, I am speaking about Taiwanese Hokkien. There's been a growing movement in recent years to acknowledge the diversity of Taiwan and be more inclusive of Taiwan's indigenous tribes, whose distinct languages, along with Hakka, are also considered Taiwanese languages. Taiwanese Hokkien is my mother tongue and the language I feel emotionally connected to, and where I have romanized it (such as the names I call my relatives), I am using the *Péh-ōe-jī* or POJ system, also known as church romanization. Throughout this book I also use Mandarin terms where they are more common, and I use a handful of Cantonese words I know from my time in Hong Kong. If that sounds like a lot . . . well, it is, and although I've tried my best to be accurate, if there are any errors, I take full responsibility for them.

This fear of making mistakes has prevented me from speaking Taiwanese for most of my life, because I was ashamed of my limited knowledge and lack of fluency. But as I've spent more time in Taiwan without the help of my parents, I've had to overcome this fear and learn that it is better to communicate awkwardly and imperfectly than not at all.

Thank you for taking this journey with me.

Year of the Dragon, Part 1

The cab delivers me to San Francisco International Airport just before 10:30 p.m. on the first Friday in February 2000, the eve of the Lunar New Year.

This is the first time I've gone to Taiwan for a major holiday rather than visiting my parents at Christmas or over the summer. It's a special year, too, though not because of the arrival of the millennium. Y2K isn't that big of a deal since it's the year 4697 according to the lunar calendar. What's exciting is that it's the Year of the Dragon, the most powerful and auspicious of all the Chinese zodiac animals. Guardian of the East and the sunrise, the dragon is wise yet unpredictable, symbolizing the forces of chaos and cosmic order.

Taiwanese couples and families in a long line wait patiently behind the China Airlines counter to check in for the red-eye flight to Taipei. It's the usual crowd of fleece-wrapped Berkeley engineers and Prada-toting Stanford grads returning home with a year's worth of presents in overstuffed suitcases. I mostly blend in, but my luggage is minimal—a few changes of clothes in a small black duffel bag, and a laptop computer case doubling as a purse. It's my second trip in two years; the more I go, the less I pack.

I nudge my bags forward, mentally rehearsing what to say. When I reach the counter, I hand over my passport and plane ticket. My heart beats faster, but I smile as though nothing's wrong.

The China Airlines ticket agent looks at my ticket, then at me. I notice the gray hairs beginning to sprout around his temples and his slightly oily complexion. He's a Taiwanese man in his mid-forties, speaking unaccented English, probably married with kids and an elderly mother-in-law at home, all three generations under one roof in Daly City or Hayward or San Jose. He looks at the ticket again, then his eyes meet mine. His face softens with a mixture of concern and pity, an *I-hate-to-tell-you-this* look. I strive to keep my face expressionless, even as I feel the adrenaline surging through my veins. I act as though I don't know what he is about to tell me with a sigh of administrative regret.

"I'm sorry, but . . . this ticket is for *yesterday*."

As I was getting ready for bed the night before, I looked at my ticket to confirm the flight number and late-night departure time. It had been an exhausting week; I was struggling to finish several freelance writing assignments while also working four days a week as a communication consultant at a financial services firm. I didn't have time to think about my trip until Friday, the day I was leaving. After a quick meeting in the morning, all I would have to do was send a few emails, tidy up the apartment, and pack for my week-long vacation. I was pleased that I wasn't going to be rushing up until the very last minute, as I usually was.

I took my passport out of the drawer and laid it on top of my plane ticket, which I hadn't looked at since the day it had arrived in the mail. It said: China Airlines flight 003, departing San Francisco at 12:05 a.m. on Friday, February 4, arriving in Taipei at 5:30 a.m. on Saturday, February 5.

My heart started pounding. How could I arrive early Saturday morning if the flight leaves Friday at midnight? It's a fourteen-hour flight. Then it hit me: My flight actually leaves on Thursday night. Tonight!

I looked at the clock. It was 11:46 p.m., only minutes before takeoff. Even if I were packed and ready, the most reckless cab-driver would not be able to get me from the Marina District to SFO in time.

My first instinct was to call the airline to see if I could change my ticket. Then came a stampede of negative thoughts: *What if they make me buy a new ticket? What if it costs a fortune? What if all the flights are sold out for Lunar New Year? What will I tell my parents?*

I dialed the China Airlines toll-free reservation line and braced myself for an expensive remedy. After three rings I got a recorded message saying they were closed and would reopen at 6:00 a.m. Next, I tried the China Airlines desk at the airport, but there was no answer.

Though I was wide-eyed from the adrenaline, there was nothing else I could do until morning. I sent an apologetic email to my dad saying I'd missed my flight and would try to get on the next one. Then I finally went to bed.

At 6:00 a.m. on Friday morning, groggy but determined, I called China Airlines. I explained my dilemma and complained that the itinerary was not explicit enough about flights leaving after midnight. I booked a seat on the Friday night red-eye, and feigned a tone of indifference when asking how much it would cost to change my ticket. When the agent quoted me a price difference of $50 plus a $75 change fee—payable at check-in—I sighed with relief. It wasn't nearly as bad as I'd expected.

I sent another email to my dad, saying, "Same time tomorrow . . . see you there."

". . . This ticket is for *yesterday*."

I look at the ticket agent, trying my best to maintain a calm, confident exterior.

"I know. I thought it was leaving tonight because the itinerary didn't make it clear that it was Thursday night. It's confusing." I smile innocently, as though it's really their mistake, not mine. "Anyway, I made a reservation for tonight's flight." I don't say anything about my utter panic the night before, my fear of having to tell my parents that I couldn't come, or my desperation to get onto the Friday night flight.

"Okay. Let's see." The ticket agent lowers his eyes to the computer screen, trying to spare me the bad karma of missing Lunar New Year with my relatives. A few keystrokes later, he locates my reservation and prints out my boarding pass. After the standard speech about having control of my luggage at all times, he hands my papers back to me. He doesn't ask me to pay the $50 price difference or the $75 change fee—and I don't bring it up.

I walk away relieved and amazed that I got off so easy. As I head toward the departure gate with my bulging carry-on bags, I muse that the Chinese gods of fortune must be on my side.

It's 6:00 a.m. on Sunday when my plane touches down in Taipei, on the second day of Lunar New Year. The ink-dark sky and stillness of the predawn landscape contrast with the fluorescent glow and faint buzz of activity in the international terminal of Chiang Kai-shek International Airport.

My mouth is dry from the long flight, and I'm dying to brush my teeth to get rid of the stale taste. Searching my purse in the ladies' room, I realize I've forgotten to bring toothpaste and will have to wait until I get to my parents' place, a half hour away.

The immigration hall is just as I remember it—cold and sterile with high ceilings and yellowish lighting. I'm surprised that the room isn't brightened with decorations since I know every other public space in Taiwan will be festooned with greetings on red banners, bundles of paper firecrackers, potted kumquat trees, and lucky images of coins and fish to signify wealth and abundance in the new year.

I expect the airport employees to be in good spirits, having just received their annual bonuses. After surrendering my passport and customs declaration to the immigration clerk, a petite woman with a severe haircut and no makeup, she says something in Mandarin that I don't understand.

"I'm sorry, can you say that in English?"

"Your passport is expired," she says, exhaling sharply. "Do you have another one?" She hands the offending document back to me.

My cheeks grow hot as her words sink in. I fumble for an explanation.

"No . . . I mean yes . . . but I didn't bring it with me." I rummage around in my purse to be sure. "I must have left my current passport at home."

I contemplate the dark blue booklet with the gold embossed eagle. On the outside it looks identical to my current passport, which is why I didn't think twice when I put it into my purse the night before. But as soon as I open it and catch a glimpse of my 10th grade photo—an earlier me with spiky hair and too much makeup—I know she's right. The page is stamped "EXPIRED" in big red capital letters.

"Do you have any other form of identification?"

"No." I don't want to show my battered old California driver's license because that's expired too.

"Are you a Taiwanese citizen?"

"I was born here, but I was two years old when my family moved to the US. So I guess not."

"How did you get here with an expired passport?" She eyes me as though I'm guilty of doing something very bad.

"I checked in at the China Airlines counter in San Francisco, and they didn't say anything, so I didn't know there was a problem. If they had told me my passport was expired, I could have gone home and gotten the correct one. But they didn't, so now I'm here."

"We can't let you in," she says matter-of-factly.

"But what am I supposed to do? The airline made a mistake. I made a mistake, but I didn't know it, and now it's out of my control." My voice begins to crack. What are they going to do with me? What am I going to tell my parents?

"Stand over there." She points to a desk at the far end of the line of immigration checkpoints. I pick up my bags and walk to the desk where a man in his fifties with a military buzz cut and wire-rimmed glasses addresses me in Mandarin. I ask whether he speaks English.

He continues in Mandarin. "What's the matter? You don't speak Mandarin?" He shoots me a look of disapproval before saying, in English, "What is the problem?"

I explain my situation as calmly as I can.

He looks down at me through his glasses. "This is very serious, you know. The airline will be fined $1,000 US dollars. Do you have any Taiwanese identification?"

"No, but I visited Taiwan a year and a half ago with my current passport. Isn't there some sort of computer record of my entry and paperwork?"

"We don't keep those records."

"So what can I do?"

"Unless you can prove your identity, we will have to send you back to the United States."

I can't believe this is happening. I've just spent fourteen hours getting here, and I only have one week of vacation. It's Lunar New Year, and my relatives are all expecting me. I can't possibly fly back now—or survive the loss of face.

"Can I talk to my parents? They're waiting for me in the arrival hall."

"You can't go outside this area."

"But they need to know what's going on. Can you send someone to talk to them?" I know my parents woke up before dawn to meet me here, as they always do. I picture them standing in the waiting area behind the glass barrier, craning their necks to see the arriving passengers emerging through the double doors.

"Follow this man. He'll take you to the transit lounge while we figure out what to do with you." They speak to each other in Mandarin. I grab my bags and follow.

The young man, a China Airlines employee, addresses me in Mandarin first, then in English. On hearing my predicament, he asks whether my passport can be sent from the States. It's a reasonable suggestion, but there's only one problem: nobody has keys to my apartment.

"Oh," he says. "You have no family there?"

He must find it hard to believe that a Taiwanese woman could live alone in another country without at least one family member, in-law, or family friend nearby. My older brother, Ted, lives in Thailand, and although I have a few cousins in the States, I rarely see them.

I consider sending my keys on the next flight to SFO, but I soon realize this isn't the best option: even if a flight left right away, it would take a minimum of twenty-four hours to get to California and back, and I'd have to get someone to collect the keys, go to my apartment, locate my passport, then redeliver the passport to the airline. Who was going to do this for me?

"Can you find my parents in the arrival hall and tell them I've been delayed?"

"I'll look for them. Please write down your father's name."

He gives me a pen and a piece of paper. I write my father's name in English: I-Jin Loh. Underneath, I start to write in Chinese characters. There are fifteen strokes in the character "loh," an uncommon surname that translates literally as "camel." I pause, trying to remember how to write the characters for my father's first name. My hand twitches, anticipating out of habit the two characters for *my* first name, which I've written hundreds of times. The young man looks at me expectantly, his hand outstretched. I feel my cheeks redden as I realize that I don't know how to write my father's name. Instead, I write down an approximation—two Chinese characters that I believe are phonetically similar.

I hand the paper back to the young man. "This is what his name sounds like in Taiwanese, but I don't know how to say it in Mandarin. These aren't the correct characters, but the sound is close."

"He has white hair," I add, just in case.

My face burns. Even though I took Taiwanese lessons during my last trip to Taiwan, I can't even write something as simple as my father's name. Since my relatives all speak Taiwanese with each other, I don't know how my father's name is pronounced in Mandarin, the official language of business and government. The language barrier shuts me out, making me no better than a foreigner. A failure.

Fifteen minutes later, the young man returns. He says he

made an announcement on the PA system, but no one responded. I plead with him to try again. In the meantime, I've located one of my dad's business cards with his name written in Chinese. I show it to him, and he chuckles.

"That's really different," he says.

A half hour later, the young man tells me he's found my parents. He noticed a dignified man with white hair, accompanied by his wife.

"Can I talk to them?"

"You cannot leave this area. But I gave them the phone number in here, so they can call you."

A few minutes later, my dad calls the transit lounge. The clerk behind the desk hands me the phone.

"Gracie? Are you okay? What happened?"

He sounds concerned but not panicked. As I tell my dad the situation, my grown-up composure seeps away. Though comforted by their presence, I'm also embarrassed by the implication that I need to be rescued. We hang up when the young man says they'll allow us to meet "across a bar."

He takes me down a long hallway to a Staff Only door, a shortcut to the arrival hall. My dad is wearing a blazer and plaid scarf, and my mom is dressed in a knee-length black coat and a red scarf. Her eyes are red and swollen. We talk for a few minutes, under supervision, in a small area sealed off by metal barriers. Though we aren't separated by glass, it feels as humiliating as a prison visit. *Hi Mom, hi Dad, this is your successful, responsible, thirty-one-year-old daughter who can take care of herself.* Even though my parents are calm and understanding, I fight back tears. Before we part, my dad hands me some phone cards to call the US. He says they'll wait for me while I try to find a solution.

The young man points me to the pay phones. I sigh and wonder who to call. It's like being locked out of my apartment, only this time I've managed to lock myself out of an entire country.

The pay phones are at the intersection of two windowless hallways illuminated by long rows of backlit advertising posters. Panel after panel portrays Taiwan's business face—a sober constellation of cell phones, computer chips, pharmaceuticals, luxury hotels, and multinational consulting firms. A dull strip of gray-brown carpet extends in each direction, worn smooth by the footsteps of thousands of arriving and departing travelers each day.

Who should I call first? What time is it? I quickly calculate: it's 7:00 a.m. Sunday in Taipei, so 4:00 p.m. Saturday in San Francisco. I dial the number for my landlord.

"Hi, this is Grace Loh, your tenant at Buchanan Street. I have a problem, and I really need your help. I'm calling from Taiwan . . ."

I babble into his answering machine, but I know it's futile. He never returns calls right away. Although I see him from time to time, double-parked in front of the building in his champagne-colored Land Rover, he's not very accessible.

I call directory assistance and get the number for Warman Security, the locksmith I called last time I was locked out of my apartment.

"Hi, I need the locksmith to let someone into my apartment. It's urgent. I'm calling from Taiwan . . ."

The receptionist says she'll page him and asks for my phone number.

"But I'm halfway across the world! Are you sure he'll call me back?"

She assures me that he will, so I repeat the numbers carefully: 011 for international, 886 for Taiwan, 02 for Taipei, and then the eight-digit number of the pay phone where I'm standing in a deserted hallway at Chiang Kai-shek International Airport.

I hang up the phone. Now what? I look down the hall at the stream of passengers coming through—tourists, students, and businessmen who've just arrived from Kuala Lumpur. They drift toward me, pulling suitcases and small children behind them. The hall echoes with the noise of a hundred people filing past me. Minutes later, the hallway is empty again.

The phone rings. It's the locksmith. I can't believe he actually called back.

"Hi, I'm calling from the airport in Taipei, Taiwan. I need you to let someone into my apartment in San Francisco . . ."

"Whoa, we can't do that. We can't just let some stranger into your apartment if you're not there."

"But this is an emergency! I'm stuck at the airport. The only way I can get out is to have someone get my passport and send it to me."

"I'm sorry, miss, but we can't help you. Too many liability issues."

I slam the receiver down and feel my eyes welling up. How did I end up like this—with no family nearby, no neighbors or friends who can bail me out in an emergency?

Actually, there *was* someone in my life that I had counted on, someone I had trusted like family, who would be there for me if I ever needed him. But I had broken up with him six months ago. Even though I was the one who had ended it and we both started seeing other people, in that moment a familiar sadness washes over me. John would know what to do, but I can't call him now, not after what I had done to him. I feel scared and alone, trapped by my mistakes upon mistakes.

Wrong passport. Wrong language. Wrong person. Wrong. Wrong. Wrong.

It's been months since I talked to John, but I remember his phone number. Not knowing what else to do, I call him, trying my best to sound normal, conversational, unhurried, even though the phone card is depleting before my eyes.

"[10] Hi, John. It's Grace. How are you? I'm calling from Taiwan."

"(Pause.) Come on. You're not in Taiwan. [9]"

"No really, I am. I'm stuck at the airport. I accidentally got on the plane with my expired [8] passport and now they won't let me through immigration until I can get my new passport sent to me."

"Oh no! So what [7] are you going to do?"

"I tried calling my landlord, but he's not there, of course. I called the locksmith, but [6] he says he can't let someone into my apartment without me there. I was wondering if maybe you could help me [5]."

"I guess . . . But I don't really know what I can do."

"I was thinking you could call the locksmith, [4] too, and explain that you're a friend and you're trying to help me. Maybe you can persuade him . . . [3]"

"(Pause.) Okay. Whatever. Who do I call?"

"Warman Security. Hey, my [2] phone card is about to expire. If we get cut off, I'll call you right back, okay?"

"Okay. [1]"

"I'm sorry. I really appreciate this. I don't know what else to do. Uh oh, my time is up [0]."

The expired phone card pops out of its slot. I have one left.

Since I've called everyone I can think of, there's nothing else to do but wait. I retreat to the China Airlines transit lounge, an airless, rectangular room with bright fluorescent lighting and a row of molded plastic chairs facing a wall of glass overlooking two of the departure gates. In the center of the room is the transit desk, a long, shiny counter painted an unappetizing shade of salmon pink, like bad suburban nail polish. Several arrangements of roses and baby's breath decorate the counter, and I can smell the one nearest me starting to decay.

I try to make myself comfortable. I take off my jacket and lay it on top of my duffel bag, then I throw a shawl over my thin gray-blue sweater to keep warm. I wipe a disposable wet towel across my face and find a barrette in my purse to put my now-greasy hair in a ponytail. I powder my face and fix my lipstick, a simple but comforting ritual.

What I really want to do is brush my teeth, but there's no place to buy toothpaste, and I don't have any Taiwanese money anyway. I ask one of the China Airlines employees behind the counter if she has a mint or some gum.

"*Ni yao shen me?*" She doesn't understand me.

I pretend to unwrap something and put it in my mouth. I ask if she has any candy—anything. She gives me a suspicious look then tosses me a piece of hard candy from a neglected candy bowl behind the counter. The strawberry-flavored candy is sticky and sweet in my mouth—not exactly breath freshening, but better than nothing.

A while later I ask the young man who helped me before if he has any gum. He gives me a pink strip of Extra Classic bubble gum. It's limp from being carried in his pocket, but I take it anyway. Of all the people I've encountered so far, he speaks English the best, and he seems genuinely sympathetic.

"What's your name?" I ask.

"Chih-ming. But you can call me Jimmy." He smiles.

"Can I plug in my computer around here? Is there an internet connection I can use?" I was hoping to find a home phone number for my landlord.

He tells me that I can take my computer to the China Airlines business center. It's in another part of the airport, so he'll have to escort me there since I'm not allowed to wander freely.

We go up to the next floor, through the departure lounge. It is buzzing with people, full of noise and color and activity, unlike the sterile transit lounge I have been waiting in. Even this early, people are buying their allowances of duty-free cigarettes and liquor, along with last-minute gifts and snacks and coffee in the airport bars. TVs are blaring the news; mothers are calling to their children; businessmen are checking in with their assistants via cell phone. I'm tempted to stay in this area instead just to be around other people, to be able to buy a snack, to browse among the souvenirs that I have no intention of buying. But I keep following Jimmy, up and down staircases, around corners, until we get to the business center.

The Dynasty Lounge looks like a hotel lobby with golden lighting, Persian rugs, and a towering arrangement of orchids on a cherrywood table. The neatly dressed receptionist glares at me while he explains to her that I need to use the computer for a while. I obviously don't look like their usual clientele.

He leads me to a small work area where I can plug in my laptop, then he disappears for a while.

I type my landlord's name into a search engine, but the results come back "no matches found." I try a different search and get the addresses of half a dozen apartment buildings in San Francisco—but still no phone number. Screen after screen turns up nothing, so I search his last name only to see if he has relatives in the Bay Area. Two names come up: Rita M. in Santa Rosa and Christine M. in Corte Madera. I know my landlord has an elderly mother in Santa Rosa, but she's in poor health, so I pin my hopes on Christine.

Jimmy escorts me back to the transit lounge and tells me that my parents called while I was gone. They're still waiting for me in the arrival hall. A few minutes later my dad calls again.

"Gracie? Where were you? Were you able to contact anyone?"

"I went to the business center to use the internet. I was trying to find another phone number for my landlord, but all I could find was one of his relatives."

"Is there anyone else you can call?"

"My ex-boyfriend's willing to help, but I don't know how I'll get him inside my apartment."

"How long do you think it will take before you find a solution?"

"I don't know. Why don't you go home and call me in a couple hours?"

"No, no . . . We'll stay here and wait for you."

I feel bad that they're missing church because of me. Some of the people in the congregation probably know that I'm coming back for the holiday, so all three of us are conspicuous by our absence. After church, we're supposed to have lunch with our relatives at the house of my dad's eldest sister, whom I call Tōa-ko· (Number One Aunt). I have a feeling we'll miss that too.

"Can you ask if they'll accept a fax of my passport? Then maybe I could leave now and come back tomorrow when my real passport arrives."

"I doubt they will let you do that."

"But there has to be something else I can do. I mean, the airline made a mistake too! They should be more understanding."

"That's just their policy."

"Can you call the US Embassy? They'll vouch for my citizenship, won't they?"

"It's not really an embassy."

I forgot that Taiwan doesn't have "official" diplomatic ties with the US or any country that has a formal relationship with mainland China.

"You know what I mean—the equivalent of the embassy. The diplomatic office."

"I don't think it's a good idea."

"All right," I sigh. "Call me back in a while."

I ask Jimmy why the airline isn't being more flexible.

"It's the airline's fault that I'm here without my passport. It's a simple mistake. I'm not hiding anything. Why can't they be more understanding?"

"It's not our decision to let you in or not. Our law does not allow anyone to enter who does not have a valid passport. We can't make any exceptions."

I nod without looking at him. Uh huh.

"Did you find someone to get your keys?"

"I'm working on it. My landlord isn't home, so I'm trying to reach someone else."

He puts his hand on my shoulder and looks me in the eye. "You know, your passport needs to be sent here on the next China Airlines flight from San Francisco to Taipei. It leaves at midnight." I nod.

"If you are here for more than twenty-four hours and your passport hasn't arrived, then we have no choice but to send you back to the States."

I swallow hard. "I'll do my best."

"Do you know how much time you have?" He points to the clock. It's almost 11:00 a.m.

"I have until three o'clock, right? Three o'clock is midnight there."

"That's right—but your friend should get your passport to the airport by ten."

I have a little more than two hours.

I go back to the pay phones and call Christine M. I'm not even sure if she's related to my landlord, but it's worth a try.

"Hello?" A woman answers. I talk fast, trying to maximize the phone card. I've used four so far.

"My name is Grace. You don't know me, but I rent an apartment from Albert M. in San Francisco. I have an emergency, but I can't get a hold of him."

"My dad's in Lake Tahoe this weekend. What do you need?"

"I'm locked out. Actually, I'm stuck at the airport in Taipei, Taiwan, because I accidentally brought my expired passport instead of my current one. They won't let me through immigration."

"Oh my god! So what can you do?"

"I need to get someone into my apartment to get my current passport and send it to me. I called your dad first because no one else has a set of my keys."

"Wait a minute, I used to have a spare set of keys for your building. Let me think . . ."

"I changed my keys last summer. I don't think you have the new ones."

"You poor thing! How are you going to get your passport?" From the sound of our voices, you would think she's the one in trouble, not me. She is breathless with panic—yet she seems to enjoy the drama, too, like a spectator driving by a car accident.

"The locksmith said he wouldn't let someone into my apartment without me there. Since your dad's not around, I thought maybe he could call the locksmith and authorize him to go in."

"What's the name of the locksmith? I'll try calling him. Call me back in five minutes, okay?"

I breathe a sigh of relief. At last, someone who can open a door for me.

I call John back and tell him I might have found a way for him to get in.

"Where's your passport? How am I going to find it?"

"I'll call you and tell you where to look. It's probably in one of the drawers in the tansu."

I call Christine back, but the line is busy.

I go back to the transit lounge for a few minutes. A China Airlines employee waves at me—my parents are on the phone. I tell them I'm close to solving the problem, and they agree to stay at the airport a little longer, until I'm sure my passport is on its way.

When I call Christine back, she tells me she can't leave the house because she's watching the baby, but her husband Joe will drive to San Francisco to meet John and the locksmith at my apartment.

"He's really going out of his way to help you, you know. In return for the favor, my husband wants a Rolex watch, and I want a pair of ruby cabochon earrings!"

I'm not sure if she's joking. She keeps me on the phone for a while, asking for more details about how I got to Taiwan. She sinks her teeth into my story as though it's a juicy bit of gossip. I imagine her shaking her head in disbelief, safe and smug in her Corte Madera kitchen.

"If I were in your situation, I'd sure want someone to do this for me!"

I go back to the transit lounge, and my dad's on the phone again. I tell him that I've arranged for someone to send my passport to me from San Francisco, and he and my mom should go home now. They've been waiting for me in another part of the airport for more than five hours.

It's barely 11:00 a.m., but I feel like I've been awake forever. My body feels heavy but strangely hollow, the way it does after I've stayed up all night writing or working. It has its own clock, oblivious to the external cues that tell me it's only mid-morning, that it hasn't been that long since I last slept or ate. Yet it feels like a different day from the day I got off the plane. Why is my stomach growling? Am I really hungry or just responding to the smell of soy sauce and meat drifting down the hall?

I decide to go to the departure lounge to see if I can get something to eat. I've also used up all the phone cards my dad gave me.

Upstairs in the departure lounge, it's a different world. It feels like walking from a library into a casino—everything is louder, brighter, in motion. Suddenly I'm surrounded by cigarette smoke and cell phone conversations and overstuffed duty-free bags. Middle-aged men in suits and young women carrying designer handbags swarm around me. Everyone is moving—either leaving or arriving. In an hour, all these people will be gone and replaced by another wave of travelers. More coming, more going.

At the nearest gift shop, I ask the cashier if I can buy a phone card. She points me to an old lady sitting at a counter at the back of the store. I walk back there and point to the phone cards on display under the glass. I hold up two fingers. The old lady, a plump grandma with short gray hair and dark penciled-in eyebrows, looks at me and says a few words in Mandarin. I shrug. She smiles and repeats her words in Taiwanese, but I still don't know what she's saying, so I say in English, "Sorry, I don't understand." She gives a little laugh and a sigh, not seeming to mind.

"You wan' phone ca?"

"Yes. Two cards."

"Okay." She mumbles something in Taiwanese and walks away for a minute while I get my wallet. She comes back holding a large, individually wrapped almond cookie, the kind you get as an airplane snack.

"You take!" She hands it to me with the two phone cards and smiles. I smile back, embarrassed by her kindness. I think of my own grandma and her unconditional affection toward me despite the language barrier. Perhaps this woman has a daughter or granddaughter living overseas too. Perhaps she knows, without explanation, the distance I've traveled to be here.

I walk down the hall to a generic-looking coffee shop. Plastered all over the front counter are examples of various coupons they accept—free coffee and cake, free breakfast, free lunch or dinner—presumably given by the airlines to travelers in transit. Several signs indicate prices for club sandwiches, chicken curry, pork buns, cake, soup, and other items in New Taiwan dollars (NTD) and US dollars. The US prices are rounded up to whole dollars, ensuring a fatter profit on items sold to tourists like me without local currency. I take a Vita Lemon Tea out of the beverage case and point to a plate of bí-hún, Taiwanese-style rice noodles which the counter person dishes up for me. My snack costs me six dollars, far more than the regular street price.

I retreat downstairs to the empty transit lounge and settle in one of the hard plastic chairs. Just as I'm taking a bite of my noodles, Jimmy enters with a cart full of lunchboxes. He hands one to me.

"I got you one too. Did you pay for that?"

I'm surprised at how concerned he is. Of all the people I've encountered at the airport, he's the only one who doesn't view me as a troublemaker. I thank him and say I'll eat the lunchbox later.

Album

1. The Man in the Suit (1960)

On the observation deck of Songshan International Airport in Taipei, a young man smiles at someone invisible, revealing white teeth. His shiny black hair is newly trimmed, and his horn-rimmed glasses rest on high cheekbones. In his left hand he holds an open umbrella, which looks like a giant, ten-petaled flower against the bright summer sky.

Standing directly in front of him, with her back to the camera, is his future mother-in-law, still slender in her dark, tight-fitting qipao with the high collar and little cap sleeves. She is fussing over his lapel, fastening a delicate silk flower that she made for him the night before. She also supervised the making of his first real suit, insisting on taking him to the family tailor in Xindian who makes all of the stylish dresses she wears to church.

It's important for her future son-in-law to look perfect as he embarks on this momentous journey halfway across the world.

It's his first time on an airplane, and the trip will be long— more than twenty-seven hours and three stops before the Mandarin Airways plane touches down an ocean and a continent away at La Guardia International Airport in New York. There, on the other side, he will meet up with his future wife, who has already been studying at Princeton for one year. She has been waiting for her sweetheart for so many months; she has so much to tell him about America. At the same time, she can't wait to speak Taiwanese again, to catch up on family gossip, to unwrap the sweets and gifts he has brought her from home.

In another photo, he is standing on the rolling stairway that leads to the plane's door. Halfway up, he turns and with his free hand makes one final wave to a crowd of friends and relatives who've come to see him off, enough people to fill several taxis. He looks like a young ambassador, poised in his new suit, palm raised as though taking an oath or baptizing a new convert. His smiling eyes show no fear; he seems comfortable with this new mission, this scholarship to study Western theology at one of the world's most prestigious seminaries.

In a few minutes he will take his last breath of the fragrant humidity of Taipei, committing to memory the mountainous landscape and the proud faces and farewell wishes of his five brothers and four sisters, his mother and father, and countless others. He will leave this sea of familiar faces and go to a city and country where he knows no one except his college sweetheart. He will train his tongue to speak a new language, adjust to using plates and silverware instead of bowls and chopsticks, and eventually learn to drive a car. Together, the young couple will begin a new chapter in their lives—their American education, their first experience of the world outside of this sweet potato-shaped island. It is the first of many migrations my parents will make.

2. The Grotto (1960)

She stands in front of a large glass window framed with white lace curtains. Her face is scrubbed clean, and she is smiling and squinting in the bright afternoon sun. Her crisp white dress and apron contrast with her long black hair, pulled back in a ponytail. Behind the window, next to a potted plant, is a refrigerated case filled with desserts and pies. The name of the restaurant is painted onto the window in a graceful arch: "The Grotto: Italian American Cuisine." Below, on the windowsill, a handwritten sign announces: "MUSSELS TO-DAY." It's a classic photo, a young woman proud to be working at her first job, eager to do well and move beyond her humble beginnings. The only surprise, among the Italian accents and the smell of basil and tomatoes and pizza dough, is her Taiwanese face.

Working at The Grotto was a way to support herself while studying at Princeton Theological Seminary. She arrived in New Jersey in 1959, a year ahead of her fiancé, who was delayed by a year of compulsory military service from which he was ultimately excused. Though she had majored in foreign languages at National Taiwan University, she spoke English haltingly and avoided unnecessary conversations until her confidence grew. Despite her shyness, she managed to get a waitressing job not long after she arrived at a respectable Italian restaurant just off of Nassau Street. She chose the English name "Lucy," inspired by the *I Love Lucy* TV show.

Initially, she had a hard time pronouncing some of the Italian words. She couldn't tell manicotti from cannelloni and would simply try her best to repeat what the customer said to the kitchen staff, whether she understood the meaning or not. "Ma-ca-ro-nee." "Spu-mo-nee." "Lin-gwee-nee." Even more amusing to her than the multi-syllabic Italian entrees was "succotash," the word they used for a side order of peas, carrots, and corn.

She learned to like spaghetti, even though the noodles were not at all like the ones she ate in Taiwan. Italian pasta was denser and came in infinitely more shapes and sizes. The superficial resemblance made her yearn even more for the tastes of home: bí-hún rice noodles, buckwheat soba, chewy ramen, and meat-filled dumplings in broth rather than cheese ravioli in red sauce. The scent of chopped garlic transported her to her mother's kitchen, where its aroma mingled with ginger and green onion would perfume the whole house whenever her mother cooked.

Her own efforts at cooking were minimal at best since she lacked a proper kitchen in the small room that she rented during her first year at Princeton. She took advantage of the free meals at The Grotto or ate in one of the dining halls on campus most days. Her wages from waitressing didn't buy much, so she learned to be thrifty, though she allowed herself the occasional splurge, like a new pair of pantyhose from Woolworth.

Years later she would occasionally visit The Grotto with her husband and children and greet her old employers. Her foray into Italian cuisine proved useful in her assimilation: she regularly cooked spaghetti with Ragu for her two kids (something her mother never made for her), and she developed a lasting appreciation for a good, old-fashioned, unadorned slice of pizza.

3. White (1962)

All of their wedding photos were lost in the mail on the way to or from the photo processor except for a few shots taken by friends and acquaintances, like this black-and-white three-by-five with a dainty, white scalloped border. The bride stands in the center, overexposed in her long-sleeved white wedding gown and veil, holding a bouquet that looks like a head of cauliflower. The dress—a lacy, poufy "wedding-cake" number that's a bit loose around the bodice—is rented. Or was it borrowed?

It must have been difficult getting married so far away from home and without the frills or fanfare she might have expected in Taiwan where she's the eldest daughter of a well-to-do family. Her attentive, stylish mother surely would have fussed over her, designing the gown and veil herself, handmaking exquisite corsages of silk orchids and peonies and arranging a ruinously lavish banquet. But at Princeton, she's just another graduate student, working part-time at the library to help support her now-husband, who's getting his PhD in biblical studies from the seminary. The full skirt of her wedding dress spreads airily around her, an illusion of lightness concealing layers of obligation. Her hair is newly cropped in a soft, curly hairdo like her mother's, signifying her change in status. She's wearing a pearl choker, the only thing she'll take home at the end of the day. If her mother couldn't oversee the entire wedding, she would at least make sure that her daughter walked down the aisle with her own jewels, head held high.

Standing next to the bride, the groom is grinning toothily in his square-framed black glasses and dark suit, handsome as a poet. (Is that the same suit he wore when boarding the airplane to go to America, waving like a celebrity to those he left behind?) His hair is still inky black, not yet prematurely gray from burning the midnight oil. His smile is open and candid, while the bride resembles the Mona Lisa, smiling inwardly at some amusing secret. Perhaps she is anticipating the reactions of friends and relatives back in Taiwan when they see the wedding photo: they will shake their heads, amazed at her courage in going away for so long, living among foreigners, eating bland American food, mastering English well enough to get a job, and getting married in such modest circumstances—away from the comforts of family and community, and yet with infinitely more freedom than any of them could possibly imagine.

4. Liberty (1962)

She stands in front of the Statue of Liberty, Liberty Island, New York. The photo is shot slightly from below to accommodate the massive statue with the spiky crown, monumental arm thrust skyward, torch cut off at the edge of the frame. She is squinting off to one side, the sun highlighting the regal curve of her cheekbone. She's wearing a long-sleeve white blouse with a wild froth of ruffles cascading from shoulders to mid-chest, and a slender bow tied at her neck. Her hair is chin length, permed into large springy curls that frame her face, unlike the long, straight tresses she wore in a ponytail or a librarian's knot when she first arrived in Princeton. This is her new, grown-up, American hairstyle, a transformation she made just before she married her husband. He's the one taking the picture.

It's their honeymoon. They are penniless graduate students, so all they can afford is a weekend in New York: the cheapest room at the Empire Hotel, a stroll in Central Park, hotdogs on Coney Island, the ferry to the Statue of Liberty. They spend a grand total of fifty dollars, beyond extravagance, the husband sweating each time he reaches for his wallet.

What is she looking at? Her eyes are focused somewhere on the distance, just like the statue in whose shadow she stands, that sentinel of American freedom, patron saint of refugees and seekers, the dark-skinned and tongue-tied. She is not smiling; she seems lost in thought, as if pondering how she came to be situated in this bright, cloudless landscape, breathing in the salty breeze of a different ocean. *Why am I here? When will I be able to go home? How will my life be different now that I'm married? Does my mother miss me as much as I miss her?*

5. Homecoming (1968)

The snapshot has a paparazzi feel to it, as though the person holding the camera wanted to capture the exact moment of the couple's dramatic entrance. Tian-Hiong is in the foreground smiling big, looking like a movie star with her sleek bouffant and cat-eye glasses. She looks thinner, more sophisticated, well-worn in a dignified way, like a leather suitcase that's circled the globe. Behind her, I-Jin looks the same but older, still handsome, with wisps of gray just beginning to show around his temples. He is smiling with his head down as someone throws a lei around his neck. This is the day they have been waiting for—the day they finally came home to Taiwan after nearly a decade studying and working in the United States.

When they left Taiwan, they were hopeful college students with little more than a plane ticket and a sense of ambition. Now, they return to their homeland transformed by their accumulated acts of passage: immigration, acculturation, graduate school, first jobs, marriage, and parenthood. They are recognized for the first time as husband and wife and are proud to introduce the gathered friends and relatives to their precocious four-year-old son, Teddy, short for Theodore ("gift of God"). They have an enviable future: I-Jin is a newly minted PhD, and Tian-Hiong, radiant in her happiness, is pregnant with their second child. A girl.

The years of hardship and homesickness are over. They are no longer in transit, no longer just "passing through" until they can make their way home. Now their lives can really begin: They will dedicate themselves to teaching at Taiwan Theological Seminary and sharing the knowledge they acquired overseas. They will be faithful servants of the church. They will go back to being the good son, the successful daughter, the trusted brother, the clever sister, the respected uncle, the thoughtful aunt. They will raise their children here, surrounded by family and supported by community. This is where they belong.

6. Passports (1971)

One family, four passports, four tiny black-and-white photos taken in a hurry for an unexpected trip. We didn't want to leave Taiwan.

FATHER. Age thirty-six, clean shaven, black hair combed back, large eyes behind square black glasses. A direct and serious gaze. Regal nose, mouth set in a firm line. *Don't look back; what matters is the future.*

MOTHER. Age thirty-six, shoulder-length hair pulled back, ends curled up in a flip. Smooth skin, square face. Cat-eye glasses, brightly patterned dress, a single strand of beads around her neck. *This is for the best.*

SON. Age seven, hair neatly combed and parted over his left eye, round cheeks, slightly protruding ears. His father's nose, his mother's eyes, an American passport. *What's the big deal? Traveling is nothing new.*

DAUGHTER. Age two and a half, no longer a baby but still a toddler. Wispy hair parted in the middle and fastened with two bobby pins. Round face, round eyes. *Mommy, Daddy, when are we going home?*

Gaining Face

Several years ago my mom discovered, hidden away in a drawer, a relic from my past. I was stunned when she showed it to me, but not because of a flood of recognition. If anything, it was the opposite: the souvenir was so old—predating the earliest of my childhood memories—that I was convinced I was seeing it for the first time. My mom had found my original green card, issued to me when my family emigrated from Taiwan to America in 1971. I was two years old.

Sin-hui, the wide-eyed, chubby-cheeked toddler pictured on my green card, bears only a superficial resemblance to the adult known as Grace. Nobody calls me Sin-hui anymore—not even my parents, nor my vast collection of non-English-speaking relatives in Taiwan, who pronounce my name *gu-LACE-uh.* Sin-hui has been reduced to the middle initials *S. H.,* or simply *S.,* invisible behind my American identity. Like the card itself, my Taiwanese persona was stashed away decades ago, gathering dust, no longer useful, and not much more than a memory—until the summer of 1998.

That summer, I went to live in Taipei for three months, where I took Taiwanese language lessons, visited relatives, bought every English-language book on Taiwan that I could find, and made an effort to get to know a place and a culture that had always been foreign to me. Though I'd visited Taiwan on many occasions—and my parents had moved back there while I was in college—I had never developed a personal connection with it. I thought of it as the place my parents were from; I was an indifferent tourist, tagging along, registering only a blur of empty rituals—banquets and church services, shopping trips, and endless visits to far-flung aunts, uncles, cousins, nieces, and nephews. But this trip was different—this time I was paying attention. I wanted to feel connected; I wanted to participate.

One Sunday, my dad took me into the historic center of Sanhsia. Named for a valley where three rivers meet, Sanhsia is a district in the southwest part of greater Taipei where my dad grew up, and where my parents planned to retire. The town is famous for its old main street, lined with crumbling red-brick buildings and brimming with antique stores selling everything from large scrolls with ancestral portraits to jade statuettes to intricately carved mahogany furniture and latticework screens. At one end of the street is Qingshui Zushi (Great Ancestor) Temple, established in 1767 and renowned throughout Taiwan for its ornate temple art. The woodworking and decorating skills of local artisans were in those days put to use in the making of coffins, another of the town's main industries evidenced by several workshops displaying huge hollowed-out tree trunks on sawdust-covered floors.

We strolled down Sanhsia's main street seeking carving of another kind: I wanted to get a chop. A chop is a slender rectangular block of durable material, such as marble or stone, with one's name in Chinese characters carved on the small end. Like a monogram or handwritten initials, it serves as a compact form of identification and is used to sign contracts, leases, and licenses—as well as traditional Chinese paintings and works of calligraphy.

My dad had bought several stones for chops on his last trip to China and asked me if I liked any of them. The most appealing was a matched set of two cut from a single piece of light gray marble with streaks of white and rust, carved on top into the shapes of a dragon and phoenix—the traditional Chinese symbols for emperor and empress, male and female, husband and wife. The pair was clearly meant for a couple, so I decided to get the other chop carved for my boyfriend John.

We passed several shops with signs advertising chops and keys, but I found the convenience-store ambiance less than impressive. I didn't want my chop carved in a place that also duplicated keys—this was a process that required human craftsmanship, not automation. On the main street we found a more traditional-looking establishment that specialized in chops and printed wedding invitations and announcements. In front was a glass case displaying all kinds of uncarved chops—ivory, marble, stone, plastic, wood, etc.—lined up in rows like miniature tombstones. Behind the case was what looked like someone's living room: In the dim light I could make out several chairs, some bookshelves, a small altar with pinpoints of light from burning incense, and a folding table covered with newspaper-wrapped bundles from the market. Judging from her posture, the shopkeeper had dozed off in front of the television; a small white dog slept at her feet.

"*Thâu-ke!*" My dad called out to her, and she woke with a start, put on her eyeglasses, and appeared behind the counter, looking a bit dazed. She was a tiny old lady with short, dyed-black hair, lines on her forehead and around her mouth, and a slightly feisty manner.

My dad said that we wanted to get a chop, and she took a few of the less-expensive ones out of the case and quoted a price that seemed too low—a few hundred NTD.

"Actually, we already have the stones," my dad clarified. "We just want to get them carved." I reached into my bag and carefully lifted out the cloth-covered box with the two marble stones in it and handed it to her.

"*Ouah*, they're big!" she said. "That's going to cost more." Most chops make a stamp that's about a centimeter square; these would make impressions that were a little over an inch square.

"How much?" my dad asked.

"NT$1,300 each, or two for NT$2,500," (about US$70) she replied firmly. She muttered something else that I didn't totally understand, about how these big chops were going to be more of a challenge and would require a more skilled carver than might normally be used. They spoke to each other in Taiwanese, the more familiar language of old-timers, rather than official Mandarin.

After a brief pause, my dad said, "I grew up around here. My father was a pastor." In other words, I'm not a tourist—can you cut me a deal? I wasn't used to hearing my dad try to bargain or influence people; he's normally so easygoing.

"Oh?" she said. "I was friends with a pastor's daughter. Her name was Aiko."

"That's Second Eldest Sister," my dad replied, the corners of his mouth slightly upturned.

The shopkeeper responded with a torrent of remembered details. "Ah! Is that right? I was one year behind her in school. We both sang in the choir. I'm seventy-one now, so she must be seventy-two. Her elder sister, Nobu—she was two years older, so she must be seventy-four—still lives here with her husband, just up the street there, where the medical clinic is. They paid for the rebuilding of the church some years ago."

"Yes, that's Eldest Sister," my dad said, nodding. I realized they were talking about Tōa-ko·, the firstborn of my dad's siblings and the matriarch of the Loh family.

The shopkeeper squinted at my dad through her glasses. "And you are . . . ?"

"I'm Third Son," he explained. "Eldest Sister is ten years older than me."

"Oh, you were too young back then. But look at you now, you're so old!" she chuckled, pointing to my dad's combed-back silver hair. Then, in a more business-like tone she said, "I'll do it for NT$2,400. Special price for you."

My dad looked at me. I flashed an expression that said *why not?* and he replied, "Okay."

The shopkeeper pulled out a couple of laminated sheets of paper with a variety of stamp designs. There were square and round shapes, thick and thin lettering, modern typestyles resembling Helvetica along with older styles of calligraphy, positive and negative imprints, bordered and borderless designs, and even a few stamps without names at all but images of Chinese zodiac animals or other symbols. While I looked over all the possibilities, my dad zoomed in on one particular design that he liked—a stylized form of calligraphy called seal script in which the characters look more like their original ideographs. I trusted his judgment and went for the style he selected but added that I wanted a border of the same thickness as the characters. Next, my dad wrote down the names for the two chops.

When the shopkeeper saw our surname, she sighed, "That's right. Her last name was Loh." She read my name aloud and said, "Sin-hui. Mmm, such a nice name." The compliment was directed more at my dad than me since I, of course, had nothing to do with choosing my own name. She asked when we wanted to pick up the finished chops, and my dad said we'd be back the following weekend.

"It's amazing that people can remember who they went to school with all those years ago," I said to my dad as we walked away. It had been a challenge for me to recall details about my classmates at my ten-year high school reunion—I couldn't imagine having lucid memories about them fifty or sixty years later.

"The Loh kids were well known," my dad said proudly, "because they were usually first in their class." I was gratified not so much because we'd gotten a discount but because I suddenly felt connected to the history of this place—something I'd never felt before.

When my dad and I returned to Sanhsia the following Sunday, we waited until the rain eased before going into town to retrieve the chops. From a distance we could see the shopkeeper standing behind the counter, straight and alert, hands folded in front of her, face brightened by lipstick, rouge, and powder. She smiled when she saw us; it was obvious that she'd been expecting us. Immediately she handed my dad an envelope containing the heavy chops. We took them out of the envelope and the shopkeeper gave us some paper and ink to test them. I took my chop and pressed it into the thick red paste, which looked like crushed lipstick in a little black pot.

"Press hard," my dad said as I touched the chop to the paper. My dad, who is not easily impressed, adjusted his glasses and scrutinized the inky red stamp. The outlines of the characters were bold and uniform, but the slight nicks and gaps in the impression gave it a wonderful, handmade quality. He pronounced it "very good . . . much better than the other ones I have." I couldn't wait to show it to my mom and to Tōa-ko·.

The shopkeeper beamed at us. "My son did it himself," she said, looking very pleased.

A month later, I was back home in San Francisco. I unpacked the chops along with the rest of my cherished souvenirs: a Chinese calligraphy set complete with ink, ink stone, brushes, and water pot; wood-block prints of Taiwanese folk deities; CDs of Taiwanese aboriginal music; a black-and-gold qipao with a high side slit that I bought in Hong Kong; and over forty books on Chinese and Taiwanese art, culture, and history.

I was content to be surrounded with reminders of my trip, but after only a few days, my vacation-induced euphoria was already being eroded by the day-to-day realities of deadlines, commitments, and responsibilities. After three months of carefree (and rent-free) exploration, I had to start worrying about a paycheck again. Taiwan resumed its place as an alternate universe to the one I existed in; they had always been mutually exclusive.

It was difficult to adjust to working again; business as usual felt strange and stifling. Before my trip, I did mostly commercial copywriting assignments that paid well but were far from spiritually rewarding. Now, I was no longer satisfied with being anonymous; I wanted to put more of "me" into my work.

I complained about this to my friend Philip one day at the café in the basement of the San Francisco Main Library. We'd gotten together to brainstorm ideas for a self-promotion: a clever card or booklet that would showcase his skills as a graphic designer and my skills as a copywriter. As we sat there nursing our lattés, I was suddenly inspired.

"I have an idea for a business card. Will you design it for me?" I quickly sketched a vertical layout with my chop in red ink at the top of the card and my name and information below it. Philip agreed to do the layout for me, and the next day we met again to scan an impression of the chop, choose a color to match the red ink, select a typeface, and purchase the paper.

One week later, Philip sent over a box of 500 business cards and 250 notecards, which he letterpress printed himself. The subtle texture of the card felt elegant and authoritative, and the imprint of the chop was beautifully rendered and very true to the actual stamp. I was thrilled.

After three years of freelancing, I finally had a real business card. I'd vowed to get one many times, but never got around to producing it. I knew I wanted a card with a memorable graphic identity, but the perfectionist in me couldn't decide exactly what it should look like. In a way, it was the same dilemma I faced when I was seventeen and wanted a tattoo: What symbol would accurately represent me? What mark or emblem could I live with forever that would age gracefully and not become stale over time?

The chop solved that problem for me not only graphically, but symbolically: It was proof that I'd regained my name and "face" in the country where I was born. It reminded me that my Taiwanese self hadn't been abandoned after all. Like a hidden message it was there all along, stamped into my DNA, waiting to be deciphered.

People that I give the card to often ask about the stamp: "Does this mean something?" I'm proud to tell them, "That's my Taiwanese name: Loh Sin-hui." I had found my true identity, represented by a symbol that was unique to me, that only I could own, and that would be mine forever. And it was perfect.

Year of the Dragon, Part 2

At 7:15 p.m. Pacific Time (11:15 a.m. in Taipei), three strangers meet at my Buchanan Street apartment: my ex-boyfriend John, who has canceled his Saturday night dinner plans to come to my rescue; my landlord's son-in-law Joe, who's driven forty-five minutes across the Golden Gate Bridge to help someone he's never met and probably never will; and the locksmith from Warman Security, a scruffy blond guy with a goatee and a wet cough, who's just doing his job.

I wait fifteen minutes, then call John's cell phone. The locksmith has already picked my locks and let him in. I imagine him standing in my living room, looking out the window, not wanting to sit down or stay any longer than he has to.

"Your apartment looks the same."

"Yeah . . ." The last time John was there was the night I broke up with him. He picked me up and we went out for dinner in Noe Valley. I was wearing a flirty new dress and heels since we were going to take a dance lesson at the Metronome Ballroom. We never made it.

"Where should I look?"

"It's in one of two places. See where the tansu is? In the second or third large drawer there should be some old wallets and ID cards. Do you see it?"

I hear the sound of drawers being opened and closed.

"I see the drawer, but there's no passport in here."

"Okay. There should be a black shoulder bag next to the sofa..."

"Uh huh... Got it."

"There's a zippered pocket on the back. Open it."

"Yup, here's your passport."

"Whew! I must have left it in the bag when I got back from Barcelona."

A pause. "When were you in Barcelona?"

"Over New Year's. I went with a couple friends. It was okay." I try to downplay it. The year before, I'd spent the holiday with John and his friends in New York—the only trip we ever took together.

"So now what?"

"Can you take it to the airport, to the China Airlines counter, and put it in an envelope addressed to Pan Chih-ming? They need to receive it before ten o'clock your time." I spell out Jimmy's name for him.

"You're lucky you got a hold of me. I was supposed to have dinner with Philip and Jacqueline." The four of us used to go out almost every weekend, but now John and I see them separately.

"Sorry about that. And thanks for doing this for me, I really appreciate it."

I hang up and take a deep breath. It's strange to talk to him now. I'm grateful for his help, but I feel terrible asking for it. John is generous to a fault, the type who adopts stray cats and buys *Street Sheet* even though he never reads it. At the same time, he fights back if he thinks someone is taking advantage of him, like the time he spent an entire weekend composing a letter of complaint to a car mechanic who ripped him off. While I knew that he would instinctively offer help—and it's clearly an emergency—I also knew that I had hurt him deeply and was no longer entitled to his kindness. He can afford to help strangers and expect nothing in return; but helping me, his ex-girlfriend, requires him to face the possibility of rejection all over again.

I am down to my last phone card. I use it to call my parents, who had arrived home a few minutes ago. I picture them walking into the lobby of their high-rise apartment complex, still sleepy from the taxi ride, and the doorman saying to them, "Eh? I thought your daughter was coming home today." My dad will mumble an excuse. They'll spend the rest of the day explaining to various relatives and acquaintances why I'm not home, enduring the questions stoically.

"What's happening? Did you get someone . . ."

"Yeah. John got inside my apartment, and he's putting my passport on the next flight out of SFO."

"Good." My dad exhales. "What time will the plane arrive?"

"Same time tomorrow—6:00 a.m."

"Where will you sleep?"

"I don't know . . . There must be an airport hotel or something." I hadn't thought of it until now—I'm going to have to spend the night here. Will they take me somewhere? Or will I be stuck in that desolate, depressing transit lounge?

"We'll pick you up tomorrow, come home for an hour, and then go straight to Taipei, okay?"

"Do we have to go out?"

"We're invited to lunch with your uncle Jī-kū. It's his sixtieth birthday."

"Oh. Okay." I wish we could relax at home, but after all I've put them through, I can't complain.

"See you tomorrow."

"Sorry you have to come again so early . . ."

"Don't worry. Just be careful, okay? Call us if you need anything."

I hang up reluctantly. Alone again. Even though my parents are only a few miles away, we're separated by a gaping, unbridgeable distance. I had expected to see them in three dimensions upon landing here on *this* side, but except for a brief glimpse that morning, they've just been voices on the end of a phone line, shadows in another time zone. Or maybe I'm the one who's a shadow. We live on opposite sides of the globe, leading mostly separate lives, yet I take for granted that I can simply get on a plane and come over here and insert myself into this reality. I've gone back and forth so many times that I should know what to expect, and yet the transition has never felt so . . . off.

I've never spent time in Taiwan when I wasn't with my parents. They always mediate and translate for me. Without them, I lose the context I've always depended on for my visits. They're the only way I can connect with anything here—my relatives, the language and customs, the insider's knowledge of the city. The little bit of independence that I have—walking around Sanhsia or taking the bus alone to certain parts of Taipei—is based on observation, repetition, and the growing usage of English signs. But I still can't order my own food in a restaurant, let alone deal with a hostile bureaucracy without assistance. I never imagined I might have to learn to navigate Taiwan on my own. What would I do if my parents weren't here to bail me out? How would I communicate? Who would I call for help?

I go back to the transit lounge and sit in one of the hard cold plastic chairs. Now that my passport is on its way, there is nothing to do but wait. It's nearly 1:00 p.m.

My mouth is dry, and I'm dying for a mint, a stick of gum, anything to change the stale taste in my mouth. I need a shower badly. My hair is greasy, and my face is flaky from the dry air and constant re-powdering. I wish I had worn something warmer than a thin sweater and unlined pants. I could change my clothes, since I have my bags with me, but I didn't bring anything heavier. How ironic, because I felt so good about packing light this time— one jacket, two pairs of shoes, and a few wrinkle-proof outfits for a week in Taiwan. I've made this trip often enough to be able to pare down to the essentials. Only this time, I forgot something important.

The sky looks like it's getting a little darker outside, though it's hard to tell for sure because of the fluorescent lighting. This room has had the same unearthly glow since 6:00 a.m. The 747s glide back and forth outside the window, each arrival corresponding with an announcement. Osaka . . . Guam . . . Denpasar. Each aircraft disgorges its unseen human cargo, signaled by a crescendo of voices and the unmistakable sound of wheeled suitcases being dragged on linoleum. A sea of bodies moves toward Immigration, and the voices drift away as quickly as they came.

For a few hours, Henry Park keeps me company. I gratefully lose track of the time and try to forget my situation and surroundings by immersing myself in the book *Native Speaker* by Chang-rae Lee. In Henry I find a kindred spirit, another immigrant tormented by the language left behind: "When I step into a Korean dry cleaner, or a candy shop, I always feel I'm an audience member asked to stand up and sing with the diva, that I know every pitch and note but can no longer call them forth."

Like Henry, who works as a spy, I've somehow managed to infiltrate my native culture without actually taking part in it. I can feign the appearance of belonging until my speech—or lack of it—gives me away. No amount of sincerity can make up for this defect, this flaw that separates me from the people I ought to consider as my own.

My butt hurts from sitting in the plastic chair, and I keep shifting my weight to try and get more comfortable. Why don't they have padded chairs? Why don't they have a continuous bench instead of these ridiculous individual bucket chairs so that you can lie down and take a nap? There's no TV, not even a water fountain in here. "Lounge" indeed. It's worse than a hospital waiting room. There's nothing to do to pass the time except read, write in my journal, and feel sorry for myself as the day wears on.

I'm glad I remembered to bring my journal. Before long, I have filled over a dozen front-and-back pages with shaky handwriting, continuing my tradition of writing the most when I feel the worst. When there is no one to talk to, I talk to myself. My pen starts to run out of ink, so I borrow another one from one of the girls behind the transit desk.

Mid-afternoon, a China Airlines employee comes up to me and starts speaking in Mandarin.

"She doesn't understand—speak English to her!" yells a clerk from behind the desk. This I can understand. Even if I don't know all the words, I always understand the condescension.

The man leans over to get closer to me, and I can smell his pomaded hair. He pushes his glasses back on his nose and hands me a small clipboard with a piece of paper on it.

"What's this?"

"You need to pay for the room. Because you stay for tonight."

"What do you mean I have to pay? Why doesn't the airline pay for it?"

"You are responsible to pay the custody fee. Please."

I look at the clipboard and feel my face getting hot. It's an invoice for the custody fee that I'm supposed to sign. I hand it back to him.

"You can't charge me for this. I'm not here voluntarily."

"Please. You must sign."

He continues to hold the clipboard in front of my face. I stare at it and think, you must be kidding. *I'm* supposed to pay? This isn't my fault. I take a deep breath and struggle to not raise my voice as I feel a wave of hostility building in my chest.

"No. I'm not signing it. I'm not paying for anything. I'll stay right here if I have to."

The man backs away, and shrugs at the clerk behind the transit desk.

An hour later, I'm hungry again. I open the lunch box that Jimmy gave me earlier and pick at the sweet and sour pork, fried shrimp, snow peas, and rice with a pair of disposable chopsticks.

Jimmy reappears and comes over to talk to me.

"Everything okay?"

"Yeah. My passport's coming on the midnight flight from San Francisco."

"Good. Now I need to ask you something." I see that he's holding the clipboard. "You need to pay the custody fee for tonight."

I try to reason with him. "Why should I pay for it? I'm not here by choice. Why should I pay for my own hotel room when I don't even want to be here?"

"It's not a hotel room."

"Then what is it?"

"You stay in a dormitory tonight. With the other passport violations."

"What?"

"There are some other people here who have trouble with their passports. So all of you have to stay in the dormitory tonight. And it costs money."

My mouth hangs open. Jimmy is the nicest person I've dealt with so far and the only one who doesn't talk to me like he's an authority figure. I am sure that I can make him see my point.

"Don't you see how unfair this is?"

"I'm afraid you have no choice. You see, if you don't pay for this . . ." He looks me in the eye and his voice softens, "then we will have to send you back on the next flight to the States."

I feel the liquid rush to my eyes. It makes sense now: the airline sent Jimmy—the only person I seemed to listen to—as a sort of ambassador to deliver the bad news. Not only would I have to pay, but it wasn't even a private room—I was going to be herded into a dark cell with a bunch of strangers. Troublemakers. "Passport violations."

I sigh heavily. "Fine," I say, feeling choked. "How much is it?"

"Three hundred and sixty NT."

Approximately eleven dollars. I hand Jimmy my Visa card and try to blink back the tears.

The hours drag on. Soon my eyelids are drooping, and my eyes feel raw from wearing my contact lenses for so long. My back hurts from too much slouching in an unforgiving chair. My feet, wearing the same high-heeled Kenneth Cole loafers for more than twenty hours, feel like they've been permanently molded into a tip-toe position like a mannequin's. The skin on my face feels oily, but if I wash it again, the cold dry air will make it tighten and shrink until it hurts to smile. I smell like unwashed hair.

It's not that different from being on the airplane. My body is neither here nor there, neither fully awake nor relaxed. I don't feel much of anything except a frustrating inertia. On the airplane, the misery of confinement is more tolerable because it is shared, and there is always someone else with longer legs, heavier bags, a less considerate seatmate, or a more somber occasion for traveling. Here in the transit lounge, I can get up and walk around, stretch my legs a bit, and use the restroom without suffocating. But I can't lie down, and there are no blankets or armrests, nothing soft to sit on, no buttons to dim the lights, no movies or music channels, no views of mountains and sea or flight attendants handing out refreshments. And this limbo will stretch on even longer than the airborne kind; I will sit underneath this same institutional clock until the hands go around not once, but twice.

By 7:00 p.m., I'm fighting to stay awake. A nap would be good, except there's no place to lie down and no way to get comfortable on these horrible, hard plastic chairs. But I try anyway, pulling my legs up on the chair next to me and sitting sideways so that I can lean my head against the wall. I wrap my arms around my knees to keep warm. I wish I had a blanket, a pillow, anything to make this more bearable. I no longer listen to the flight announcements, which have turned into white noise, a blur of indistinguishable syllables. I try not to dwell on my envy of the people streaming off the planes, passing me on their way to the outside world, to welcoming arms, cushioned car seats, real food, fresh air.

I nod off after a while and am awakened by a China Airlines employee who says he will take me to another place where I can sleep. I groggily gather up my things and follow him down one hallway, then another, tunneling through to the deep insides of the airport, far from any windows. He brings me to another lounge, a bizarre, badly lit triangle-shaped room with dark green, faux-leather sectional seating lining two walls, and two tables in the middle surrounded by ugly upholstered chairs. On one wall there are posters of Taiwan—a city skyline, a famous temple, and the natural rock formations of Taroko Gorge. A refrigerator hums in one corner. The blue carpet is permanently stained, and the ceiling is discolored from water leaks. Despite the depressing, sixties era décor, I am glad to escape the fluorescent glare and hard surfaces of the transit lounge. At least here I can nap in comfort.

Two airport employees sit at one of the tables, watching TV and spitting pumpkin seed shells onto a sheet of newspaper. There's a man taking a nap on the far end of the sectional sofa and two other people having a conversation. I avoid eye contact and choose an unoccupied part of the cushy green sofa on which to curl up and close my eyes. I sink into the overstuffed cushions gratefully and am about to fall asleep when I hear a voice speaking in my direction.

"Hello! Where are you from?"

I reluctantly open my eyes and see a young white man in need of a haircut, looking at me with a curious expression.

"San Francisco. And you?"

"Australia. Name's Martin."

"Hi, Martin. I'm Grace."

He sits down on the floor in front of me, and I give up on taking my nap.

"So what's brought you here? Passport problem?" he asks.

I'm not sure I have the energy to hold a conversation, but it suddenly feels good to have someone to talk to, in English, who isn't judging me and just wants to listen. Before I know it, I am breathlessly recounting all the details of my ordeal to him, punctuating with lots of sighs and eye rolling. It sounds different when I tell it this way, *you-wouldn't-believe-what-happened-to-me,* than when I am trying to convince the airport officials that it's not my fault.

Martin nods sympathetically, then tells me his story. He and his girlfriend had been living and teaching English in Taiwan, and they just returned from a vacation to Bangkok. They were passing through Taiwan on their way home to Australia, stopping just long enough to pack up the rest of their belongings, when he got detained because his visa had expired. His girlfriend was able to get through and was at this moment moving all of their stuff out of the apartment while he was at the airport.

"She's coming back tomorrow, so this'll be my second night here," he says in his Australian drawl.

"Really?" I didn't know that it was possible to stay at the airport that long or to be in a worse situation than the one I was in. Now I feel sorry for him.

"Aw, that's not so bad. You see David here . . ." He points to the dark-skinned man asleep on the other end of the sofa. "He's been stuck here for two months."

My jaw hangs open. Months? Why? Martin explains that David is from Lagos, Nigeria, and arrived here without a passport so he could neither enter Taiwan nor fly anywhere else. His only option is to go home, which he doesn't want to do for political reasons. David is *really* stuck—a man without a state, whose language difficulties and cultural isolation are far more acute than mine. I look over at David, feeling embarrassed about my trivial-by-comparison story, and see that he's not actually asleep. My eyes meet his for a moment; they're bloodshot and weary. I force a smile.

Martin keeps me entertained for a while, telling me about his new job at Andersen Consulting, which surprises me because he looks like a bohemian backpacker, not a management consultant. A while later, Jimmy pokes his head in to check up on me.

"Everything okay? Your passport's coming?"

"Yeah, it'll be here in the morning. Thanks for all your help."

He says he's finally going home after working a double shift—from 5:00 a.m. until 10:00 p.m. I wonder if that's a normal schedule for him or if he stayed overtime to make sure that I was going to be okay. It's Lunar New Year after all, and he should be spending it with his family.

Around 11:00 p.m., a guard rounds us up and escorts us to the dormitories. We follow him even deeper into the bowels of the airport, further from windows and natural light, several thresholds away from the outside world. Martin, David, and two other male detainees are shown into the men's dormitory. Me and the other female "passport violation," a quiet woman with coffee-colored skin, are led into the women's dormitory next door and told to lock the door behind us.

The dorm looks like a large, sterile hospital room. Or a room in a movie orphanage. The paint is peeling, and the walls are slightly stained. Everything is white, the color of mourning. Seven twin beds, covered only with a thin white sheet, are lined up against the walls along with seven identical white nightstands. The headboards and nightstands are each painted with a number from one to seven, arranged in no particular order. There are no chairs or shelves or tables in the room, no TV, nothing else except an ugly oversize clock on the far wall and a page torn out of a 1997 wall calendar taped next to it.

I put my duffel bag down on bed number four—my lucky number, but Taiwanese people consider it unlucky. I pull open the drawer on the nightstand and find a pillow and a tan army-style blanket, which I unfold on the bed. It smells like mothballs. The other woman shuffles in behind me, dragging her wheeled, tapestry suitcase behind her. She sits down on the edge of bed number three, on the other side of the room. I half smile at her, trying to be neighborly, but she ignores me. She appears to be in her late twenties or early thirties and is short and plump with curly black hair. She says nothing, and I assume that she speaks neither Chinese nor English. I wonder if she's Malaysian or Indonesian, here to seek work as a domestic helper to an upper-middle-class family in Taipei.

The room is unbearably cold, so I go over to another night-stand and pull out an extra blanket and pillow for myself. The woman opens up her suitcase and pulls out a large colorful piece of cloth and spreads it out on her bed. It's one of those tie-dyed squares you buy on the beach that can be used in a million ways: sarong, shawl, tablecloth, picnic blanket, bedspread. Though in many ways she seems more lost than me (What misfortune brought her here? Will someone claim her in the morning?), I admire this little bit of wisdom on her part. I packed what I considered essential—clothes, books, and my laptop computer. She brought a piece of home with her, a thin yet precious layer of comfort. I watch as she smooths the edges of the cloth down on the bed, sits in the center of it, then swings her feet up and lies down flat on her back to sleep. She's still fully clothed, even down to her cheap white sandals, and still wearing what looks like a plastic tour group badge.

I unpack my toiletry kit and head for the communal bath-room on the other side of the room. It has two toilet stalls and two shower stalls, a large industrial sink, and a water fountain. The institutional-looking towels, plastic curtains, and cold gray tiles don't discourage me because it's been more than forty hours since I showered, brushed my teeth, or changed my clothes. Some basic amenities are stocked on the shelf above the sink, including, to my profound relief, a small tube of toothpaste.

The warm water feels good on my back; though it's late and I'm exhausted, I linger under the shower. My hair is so dirty that I have to lather it three times. The water, soap, and shampoo feel soothing and luxurious; perhaps if I stand here long enough, they'll wash away everything about the day—my mistakes and ignorance; the unfriendliness of the airport employees; the dis-appointment of my parents; the sadness I still feel about John;

and the cold, stale air. When I finally lie down to sleep, my objections fade almost instantly into complete and comforting blackness.

I reach out blindly toward the beeping sound and strain to open my eyes. All I can see are the blurred outlines of things, a bunch of blue rectangles in the dark, windowless room. Bed, dresser, bed, wall. The vague shape of another body sleeping on the other side of the room, her feet pointing toward mine. The frayed edges of my dreams dissolve, and I remember where I am. The dormitory. The airport.

Shivering, I pull off the threadbare blanket and rough sheets and sit up. The linoleum floor is cold through my socks. Apologizing silently to my roommate, I flip the light on, flooding the room in harsh fluorescence. She doesn't flinch. I have no idea if she's awake or asleep, or even what her name is.

I pull a comb through my hair, still damp from the night before, but thankfully clean. I wash my face again, taking comfort in the warm water and scrubbing hard to rid myself of any residue of what feels like a long, surreal dream. Quickly, I pack my things, ridding the room of any evidence of my stay. I notice graffiti on the dirty white walls, in English and Chinese, and decide against leaving any trace of myself.

I slip my feet into my shoes and wince at the familiar ache. Luggage in hand, I head for the door, only to find that it's locked from the other side. I drop my bags and pound on the door with my fists.

"Hello! Hello! Let me out!"

There's an armed security guard sleeping on a cot wedged up against the door. I keep pounding, not caring if I wake up everyone else too. Muffled noises come from behind the door, and a groggy voice mumbles something in Mandarin.

"Let me out! It's time!"

The hideous clock on the other side of the room reads 6:18 a.m. The flight from San Francisco should have arrived by now. The flight with my passport on board, in a sealed envelope, with PAN CHIH-MING written in John's square handwriting.

A key turns in the lock, and the door opens a crack. I see a cot covered with the same kind of moth-eaten blankets used in the dormitory. The guard is buckling his belt over baggy pants and cursing me under his breath. He shoots me an accusing look, as if to say, *What's the hurry, miss?*

I push the door all the way open, causing the cot to scrape across the floor. My body is tense like a coiled spring, every cell focused on a single goal: getting my passport and getting out. I know he doesn't speak English, but I say it anyway, in a tone of exaggerated urgency.

"Hurry up! Let's go! I'm going home NOW."

The Pig Festival

I was awakened at eight o'clock on a holiday morning by what sounded like sirens in the street beneath my parents' fourth floor apartment in Sanhsia. The piercing melodies of a Chinese trumpet orchestra were being pumped out of loudspeakers mounted on a truck, and to my unaccustomed ears they sounded as shrill and tuneless as a chorus of New Year's Eve noisemakers.

The commotion signaled the beginning of the parade that my parents had planned to take me to see, but we had overslept and missed the procession. I tiptoed out of the tatami room in my pajamas, not wanting to wake my parents yet, and made myself a cup of instant coffee in their cramped kitchen.

A few months earlier, when I told my dad that I wanted to visit Taiwan during Lunar New Year, he said, "Good! There's a special festival in Sanhsia during that time and we can go together."

Every year, he explained, several prominent families in the Sanhsia area compete to see who can raise the fattest pig. On the sixth day of Lunar New Year, the fattened pigs are paraded around town on the backs of trucks and then displayed in front of Qingshui Zushi Temple, famous throughout Taiwan for its exquisite sculptures and ornate temple art. Officially called the Seven Families Festival but more prosaically referred to as the

Pig Festival, Sanhsia holds one of the biggest events in Taiwan, making it a popular attraction for sightseers from Taipei and other nearby cities.

I was excited to see the Pig Festival partly because it was in my dad's hometown and partly because I had always wanted to observe a Taiwanese holiday celebration up close. My previous visits to Taiwan had never coincided with any major festivals except for Ghost Month, the late summer observance that honors the dead with burned paper money and ceremonial food offerings. My parents and relatives never took part in these rituals; as Christians they did not celebrate holidays other than Christmas and Easter, and they dismissed the beliefs underlying these traditions as superstition. While I maintained a certain distance from these practices, like my parents did, I was still curious about them because I hadn't lived in Taiwan since I was two years old, and I yearned for more experience with Taiwanese culture.

I knocked on my parents' bedroom door around nine thirty, and they joined me in the living room for a breakfast of sweet rolls, coffee, and the morning news. As usual, the news was dominated by stories about Taiwan's upcoming presidential election and the three leading candidates: Lien Chan of the Kuomintang party (KMT), independent candidate James Soong, and former Taipei mayor Chen Shui-bian of the Democratic Progressive Party (DPP).

After a couple of days of watching Taiwanese news and quizzing my parents, this was what I understood about the election dynamics. Lien, currently serving as vice president under Lee Teng-hui, was a safe but unexciting choice for the ruling KMT. Despite its history of repression and corruption, the KMT was still by far the largest, richest, and most powerful party, and polls had shown a majority of Taiwanese favored the status quo over the risks of political change. Soong had been a high-ranking KMT official until he went his own way after losing the party's nomination to Lien. With a solid political base and a more charismatic personality than his rival, he was considered a genuine threat to the KMT even though he declared his candidacy without any party affiliation.

In my parents' eyes, Soong offered no significant differences in ideology from the KMT since both were open to eventual reunification with mainland China. I knew that the only candidate they would consider voting for was Chen Shui-bian because of his ties to the Taiwan independence movement. Chen had created a name for himself as the youthful, vigorous, and populist mayor of Taipei, where he cleaned up city streets and streamlined the bloated administration of his KMT predecessors. But his pro-independence views were controversial; mainland China portrayed him as a troublemaker and threatened military action if Taiwanese voters chose a "separatist" candidate.

By the time my parents and I were ready to go out, it was ten thirty. We'd missed the parade, but there was still time to see the winning pigs on display in the temple square, a ten-minute walk from my parents' apartment. Although my mom and dad have lived in Sanhsia for many years after they moved back to Taiwan from Hong Kong, they had never paid much attention to the festival until this year.

"It will be very crowded," my dad warned. "It's best not to carry a purse." I stuffed a few hundred NTD into the pocket of my black microfiber jacket and grabbed my camera, careful to wind the strap securely around my wrist. My dad zipped up his parka, my mom knotted a silk scarf around her neck, and then the three of us walked into town.

We turned left onto the main drag, Zhongshan Road, where dozens of street vendors had set up temporary booths for the holiday. Carts filled with stuffed animals, cheap nylon jackets, cell phone accessories, pirated music CDs, handbags, hats, scarves, and various kinds of fruit and snacks lined each side of the street. Walking single file between the carts and moving vehicles (sidewalks are considered superfluous here), we made our way to Ren Ai Road and turned right, near the entrance to Tōa-ko·'s house and my cousin's dental clinic.

"This way," my dad said, pointing across the street. "There's a shortcut to the temple." We entered a narrow alley lined with crumbling brick and cement houses. A thin, elderly man with sun-browned skin and a bent back was sweeping in front of one of the run-down dwellings. My dad stopped to ask if this alley would lead us to the temple.

The old man looked us over and nodded. Seeing our cameras and city clothes, he said in a tobacco-tinged voice, "*Lí Tâi-pak lâng. Góa khòaⁿ-tióh tō chai* (You're from Taipei. I knew as soon as I saw you)." I was pleased that I knew enough Taiwanese to understand him, even if his comment was a slight insult.

We followed the smell of burning incense and barbecued meat down another alley, and we finally emerged in the south-west corner of the temple square, where we were greeted by more high-pitched Chinese trumpets, clashing cymbals, the pop-pop-pop of firecrackers, and festive crowds.

The first thing I noticed was an explosion of color—red, magenta, green, and gold—from the row of decorated trucks parked in the square. The back of each truck held an elaborate metal-framed façade with flashing lights, mirrors, and hundreds of small moving parts, like a gigantic pachinko machine. I thought of Antonio Gaudí, whose whimsical and vaguely psyche-delic architecture I'd recently seen in Barcelona. Underneath the neon splendor of the façades, the main compartments appeared like theater stage sets with elaborate carved panels framing the edges of a large round opening for the pig. I slipped my camera out of its case and took a few pictures.

The crowd was growing by the minute; people on every side of me were craning and jostling to get a better view of the prize-winning pigs. Toddlers balanced on their fathers' shoulders; one little boy in a red jacket put his hands over his ears to drown out the din of trumpets and exploding firecrackers. My mom grabbed my hand so we wouldn't be separated and put her other hand over her mouth to avoid inhaling the smoke from the firecrackers and incense. My dad, already several feet in front of us, became a bobbing head of silver-white hair in the pulsating crowd.

We pushed our way forward, and I got my first glimpse of one of the pigs up close. Though slaughtered early that morning, the pig skin was carefully displayed to give the illusion of a still living animal. I couldn't believe how big it was—the skin was at least six feet across, stretched over a rounded frame to make it look three-dimensional. It looked like an enormous light pink balloon with a tiny face at the bottom. Some of the pigs had their stiff black bristles shaved into decorative swirls and waves, while others had small pineapples or apples tucked into their jaws as another flourish. Bright red paper lanterns and red and blue Republic of China flags completed the garish décor.

"They're huge!" I said, catching up to my dad. "Which one is the biggest?"

"I don't know. That one is sixth place, and the one next to it is third place."

"How much do they weigh?"

"The biggest ones are over a thousand pounds, maybe fifteen hundred."

"Aiyaaah!" My mom looked at me. "So huge!"

My dad explained that the pigs are fattened up over the preceding months—some to such gross proportions that they can no longer stand on their own legs. They simply lie on their sides and eat all day. The wealthier families who participate in the competition often hire professional breeders to force-feed the pigs for them. Although the festival was undeniably unique and exciting, I was aghast at how the animals were treated.

The trucks were parked side by side, in three rows of four. We tried to get to the inner row, nearest the temple, where we thought the first-place pig would be. Apparently, there were several more pigs in decorated trucks parked in a lot on the other side of the Sanhsia bridge—the overflow. The competition has become more popular in recent years with ambitious families trying to raise their profile in the local community.

We moved forward as best we could, but there was no order to the flow of people; every person seemed to be rushing in a different direction. The crowd churned and vibrated, seeming to have an energy of its own.

"Grace!" my dad shouted over his shoulder.

"Yeah?" I struggled past a young man in a knit cap who nearly stepped on my foot.

"I think some presidential candidates may be coming here today."

"Really?" I smiled, even as I noticed a middle-aged woman wrinkling her brow at me, probably wondering why we were speaking English.

It made sense for the candidates to come to Sanhsia; the Pig Festival was photogenic and provided a perfect opportunity to press the flesh in a colorful, festive environment. The presidential election was less than six weeks away, and the local news channels documented every move made by the three frontrunners. At the time, they reported no consistent lead by any candidate. It appeared to be a three-way tie with Lien, Soong, and Chen each receiving support from roughly 25 percent of those polled, while the remaining 25 percent of Taiwanese voters remained undecided. It was shaping up to be a very close race.

Moments after my dad relayed the gossip to me, the pushing became more intense, and it was hard to propel myself forward. My mom, who had been by my side a minute ago, was now several feet behind me as people continued to squeeze between us. I was shoulder to shoulder with other determined sightseers and could no longer move independently of the crowd. As though carried by a wave, I drifted sideways, then forward, then sideways again. I gripped my camera tightly.

Several men in somber uniforms materialized in front of me. Then I noticed a couple of green and white banners moving toward me. I couldn't read the Chinese characters on the banners, but my dad recognized them immediately.

"Chen Shui-bian is here!" he shouted back to me. I could barely hear him above the noise of the excited crowd.

"Mom!" I looked over my shoulder. "Did you hear that? It's Chen Shui-bian!"

Her face lit up and she nodded in acknowledgment. More banners and several bulky TV news cameras floated toward us in the crowd. I noticed men wearing green and white windbreakers and realized those must be Chen's campaign colors. Up close, I saw the faces of Chen and his vice presidential running mate, Annette Lu, on the banners.

I was excited at the prospect of seeing the candidate my parents would vote for. They shared more than a belief in Taiwan's independent future; they were connected by a historical event that took place more than twenty years ago. Chen's political career took off in 1980 when he served as one of the lawyers for the Kaohsiung Eight, a group of prominent political activists who were arrested during a peaceful demonstration commemorating

International Human Rights Day on December 10, 1979. In what became known as the Kaohsiung Incident, dozens of protesters calling for a democratic government and an end to martial law were arrested and thrown into prison.

Among those detained were several church leaders, including my mom's uncle, Rev. Kao Chun-ming. A respected minister and general secretary of the Presbyterian Church in Taiwan, Rev. Kao was sentenced to seven years in prison and served four of them for sheltering one of the organizers of the demonstration, veteran activist Shih Ming-teh. In 1987 martial law was lifted after almost forty years (at the time, the longest period of martial law in the world), and Rev. Kao was finally released from prison. I vaguely remember going to a banquet in his honor the summer after I graduated from high school, when I visited Taiwan with my parents (we were living in Hong Kong at the time). I didn't know much about Rev. Kao's political involvement back then, but I recognized his face from photos my mom had shown me and understood that my "Great Uncle the Dissident" was a hero to many.

Another Kaohsiung defendant and political prisoner was Annette Lu, a Harvard-educated activist and feminist leader who was one of the founders, along with Chen and Shih, of the opposition Democratic Progressive Party (DPP) in 1986. The highest-ranking female in the DPP and Chen's running mate, Lu was the other face on the green and white banners inching closer to me in the teeming crowd.

We were in a narrow corridor between the parked trucks and a row of shops lining the square, about twenty feet away from the temple entrance. Chen's entourage was moving away from the temple, and it occurred to me that if he was here, he was going to have to walk right past me.

The crowd surged forward, met with resistance, then

advanced again. No one was paying attention to the pigs anymore. Someone in front of me yelled, but I couldn't understand what he said.

Looking in the direction of the news cameras, I caught my first glimpse of Chen Shui-bian. Just ten feet away, he was smiling and shaking dozens of outstretched hands. His lips were moving, but it was impossible to hear what he was saying above the commotion. At first I saw only his head—his shiny combed-back hair and square wire-rimmed glasses. Then I saw his dark gray suit accented by a bright red and gold tie—perfect for Lunar New Year. Camera flashes rebounded all around him. I reached up with my right hand and aimed my camera above and in front of me. Snap. Snap.

I turned around but couldn't see my mom anywhere. My dad was far ahead of me, his silver hair disappearing and reappearing as the crowd propelled him further away. I was only a few feet away from Chen now. I could see beads of sweat on his brow, and I noticed that he wasn't much taller than me, perhaps five foot six inches at the most. I stuck my hand out and tried to think of something to say . . . *I came all the way from California! I can't vote, but if I could, I'd vote for you! Taiwanese Americans support you!* Nothing seemed quite appropriate, and I realized he wouldn't be able to hear me above the excited voices, wailing trumpets, and popping firecrackers anyway.

The heat and noise of the throbbing crowd, which I would normally find unbearable and suffocating, felt exhilarating. It was the opposite of how I had felt just a few days ago—lonely, cold, and alienated in the trenches of CKS airport. Now I was at the center of a colorful Taiwanese festival, and an arms-length away from one of the most controversial and closely observed politicians to emerge in Taiwan's history, a man whose victory in the presidential election could spell revolution for this country of 22 million people. This time, I was in the right place at the right time.

My view was blocked by dozens of outstretched arms straining to shake Chen Shui-bian's hand. Though I was enjoying being a part of this buzzing crowd, I felt like I was going to be crushed by all the bodies pressing against me. One by one, each greedy hand was rewarded with a brief but firm shake. When Chen's fingers finally gripped mine, for a split second, I looked him in the eye and mouthed the words: *please win.*

Projections

Every March, I install myself at the Kabuki Theatre in Japantown during the San Francisco International Asian American Film Festival. It's a good opportunity to see films that will never make it to the local multiplex. It's also an educational experience for me, a way in which I try to fill the gaps in my own memory and understand my native culture and history.

I was born in Taiwan in 1969, but I've spent most of my life in the States. Though I've visited Taiwan many times, it feels foreign to me, an alternate universe that does not intersect with my American life. When I'm here in the States, Taiwan ceases to exist for me, except when I enter the realm of film. There is something magical about being immersed in a film and feeling as if I've made a true connection, even though I know it's an illusion, a dream from which I'll eventually wake. It has to do with language: While I'm used to hearing Taiwanese in Taiwan, it feels strange to hear it when I'm in the States. Though Taiwanese is my first language, I haven't spoken it since I was five, and the sound of it transports me to another world, a way of being I can barely remember.

It plays like the music of dreams, a sweet melody from childhood that is clear and complete and comforting, but it fades so quickly upon waking that you are surprised by the loss of what seemed so familiar. What was a symphony is reduced to a few haunting notes, from which you try in vain to recreate the whole. This failure brings a feeling of shock and anguish, like realizing you can't quite conjure up the face of a loved one. It is blank where there ought to be something meaningful, and—you imagine—unforgettable, and before long, you distance yourself from it, give up, as if those memories were someone else's and not your own.

*

March 9, 2000. I've been back from Sanhsia for several weeks. It's nine days before the presidential election in Taiwan, and one in four voters still remains undecided, though I know who I would vote for . . . I show up at opening night of the film festival sporting my bian mao, a funky knit cap worn by supporters of opposition candidate Chen Shui-bian, known colloquially as A-bian. I hope that a fellow Taiwanese American will recognize it and strike up a conversation, but no one does. As I settle into my seat, the lights dim, and the San Francisco Taiko Dojo begins their performance. The drumming is fast and hypnotic, each beat chipping away at the external world until I forget my surroundings. All thoughts recede except one: I think of my cousins, wishing they were here with me instead of on their way to Taiwan to attend their grandfather's funeral. And then it hits me: If all my "American" cousins are in Taiwan, that means I'm completely alone here. If China were to invade Taiwan to prevent Chen from being elected, then my entire family—including my parents—is at risk. The ocean between us—a minor obstacle before—suddenly seems unfathomable, as though I am realizing its vastness for the first time. I'm conscious again of the theatre, of being one among hundreds of Asian Americans gathered for the film festival. Normally I would feel a sense of kinship with them, but tonight they're no better than strangers. They offer me no comfort at all.

*

The film *A City of Sadness* (Hou Hsiao-hsien, Taiwan, 1989) depicts the hardships of a Taiwanese family from the end of the Japanese occupation in 1945 to the arrival of the Chinese Nationalists (Kuomintang) and Chiang Kai-shek in 1949. The two older brothers run a drinking establishment called Little Shanghai where they regularly indulge in gambling, fistfights, and women of the night. But the character I identified with was Wen-ching, the youngest brother who is as quiet and gentle as his brothers are rowdy. Born deaf and mute, Wen-ching "talks" through gestures and by writing on a notepad. Though he's able to communicate, he can't engage in a truly equal dialogue. He remains a witness and outsider, able to understand but not speak.

The climax of the film is a riot scene based on the infamous 2-28 Incident which marked the beginning of the era known as the White Terror. On February 27, 1947, a woman selling cigarettes without a permit was pistol-whipped by Kuomintang police officers, and a bystander was killed in the confrontation. The next day, hundreds of Taiwanese unleashed their pent-up anger by rioting and attacking mainlanders, recent arrivals from China whom they associated with the corrupt KMT regime. In the scene, Wen-ching and his best friend are about to board a train for Taipei when they get separated in the raging crowd. Wen-ching boards the train alone and is stopped by a couple of hoodlums looking for mainlanders to beat up. They ask him where he's from, and he stands paralyzed, eyes wide, mouth open, unable to answer. They stare at each other for a long moment, and as the thugs move in on him, Wen-ching chokes out the words: *"Góa Tâi-oân lâng!* (I am Taiwanese!)" The words sound awkward and slurred, for he has never pronounced them before. But they are magic words, and they save his life.

*

March 11, 2000. I complain to my writing group that the election I care about the most is one I can't vote in. No matter who gets elected in the US, my life won't change dramatically. But the candidates in Taiwan have radically different positions, and the safety and freedom of my relatives depends on the election's outcome. Jackie says I should write an opinion piece, but I've never done this before, and the election is only a week away. Will I find my voice in time?

March 13, 2000. I struggle with the op-ed. I'm afraid to write, but I have to write . . . silence was the curse of my parents' generation. Taiwan was under martial law; speaking out about politics could get you arrested or killed. That's why my parents had come to the States—to give me the voice they did not have. Was their sacrifice worth it? I lost my native tongue, but I gained freedom of speech. Now Taiwan is democratic, and its future depends on having the courage to speak: I am not Chinese. I am Taiwanese!

*

First Person Plural (Deann Borshay Liem, United States, 2000) is an autobiographical documentary about a Korean orphan adopted by an American family in the 1950s. Cha Jung-hee is a frightened little nine-year-old girl when she arrives in the US, unable to speak a word of English. Within months, she is transformed by the love and attention of her adoptive family. She gets over her shyness, begins talking and laughing, and gradually grows into her new identity as Deann Borshay, daughter of Arnold and Alveen Borshay of Fremont, California. She accepts her new life. She assimilates. She forgets Korea.

Over a decade later, in her mid-twenties, Deann begins to have flashbacks in which her Korean father tries to speak to her. Anxious to connect with her past, she looks through her old childhood photos that accompanied the adoption papers. A discrepancy leads her to write to the adoption agency, and a few weeks later she receives a letter that changes her life forever. She finds out that her mother, brother, and three sisters are all alive—that she was not an orphan at all. This revelation is the beginning of a painful journey for Deann—both physical and psychological.

Deann makes several trips to Korea to be reunited with her family there—what ought to be a happy occasion—but she is overcome with tears. Why is it that in addition to feeling enriched by her Korean family, she also feels bereaved?

I cried nonstop during the screening, stirred by an indefinable grief. Later, I realized that I felt Deann's sadness so deeply because in many ways it echoes my own. Why is it that thinking about Taiwan sometimes makes me feel sad when I've made so much progress in getting to know my relatives and the culture there? Because in opening my eyes to this other existence— finding this other side of myself—I am forced to acknowledge what has been lost: a family, a language, a way of life, an identity. Deann and I are mourning the same thing: the unlived life, the person who might have been, if things had turned out differently.

*

March 14, 2000. At 5:00 p.m., I submit the opinion piece. It's not perfect, but it's the best I can do in the time that I have. I meet Peggy for sushi and then we go to the film festival. She says, "good for you" when I tell her about the essay, though I know she's not as worried about the election because most of her relatives live here. I thought I'd feel relieved after submitting the piece, but I have a knot in my stomach the entire evening.

*

I've noticed a pattern in some recent Taiwanese films—including *Murmur of Youth* (Lin Cheng-sheng, Taiwan, 1997) and *Jam* (Chen Yi-wen, Taiwan, 1998)—involving the symbolic function of the Taiwanese language. In a story with otherwise Mandarin-speaking characters, there is often one Taiwanese speaker with what could be called an archetypal role.

The Taiwanese speaker is usually a plainspoken old man or woman with a peasant-like appearance—rugged, sun beaten, and lacking in refined manners and pretensions. In contrast, the Mandarin speakers are sophisticated urban types who speak in euphemisms and put on airs. The interaction between these characters is predictable in that the Taiwanese speaker will perceive something that is not immediately apparent to the other characters. He or she will comment on the events unfolding in a way that seems ignorant at first but is later demonstrated to have some wisdom. In other words, the Taiwanese speaker is the first to see the emperor's new clothes—to reveal a hidden truth that's in plain sight but unacknowledged.

The unspoken truth is a theme found in countless narratives worldwide, but I believe there's a specific meaning for Taiwanese audiences. The ultimate unspoken truth—a consensus reached without discussion, which is never explicitly stated but instinctively understood by all—is that Taiwan is independent from

China. Any movie whose plot can be summed up as "failing to see what's right under your nose" is a movie about Taiwan's dilemma: getting China and the rest of the world to recognize the reality of two separate states.

*

March 15, 2000. I check my voice mail at lunchtime, and there's a message from the op-ed editor of the *Chicago Tribune.* She wants to run my piece in tomorrow's paper! I call her to discuss details then sign and fax the contract. Next I call Shelly, my good friend in Chicago, who assures me that the *Tribune* is the "good" paper and promises to send me extra copies.

March 16, 2000. The article's up! I email friends and family with a link to the *Tribune* webpage, and within minutes my inbox fills with congratulatory messages. But my euphoria doesn't last long. I read that in a last-ditch attempt to influence Taiwan's election, Chinese Premier Zhu Rong-ji shouted in a press conference that China was "ready to shed blood to defend the territorial sovereignty of the motherland." A conflict had been hinted at before, but this was the most violent threat yet, meant to frighten the Taiwanese into not voting for Chen, the candidate most likely to seek an independent future for Taiwan. All day I feel jittery and restless, angry that the rest of the world seems to be able to shrug this off; the article wasn't even on the front page. Does anyone else realize that Taiwan and China have never been closer to war? Have people forgotten that the US is obliged to defend Taiwan if China attacks? I'm scared for my family, but there's nothing I can do. I email my dad and ask: Are you afraid? "No," he says, "they've been making these threats all my life. This is no different."

*

In *Connection by Fate* (Wan Jen, Taiwan, 1998), Ah-de, a former activist now working as a taxi driver, gives a ride to Mah-le, a young aboriginal Taiwanese on the run for murdering his cruel employer. Mah-le is apprehended and executed for his crime, but Ah-de continues to see his ghost everywhere. In Chinese legend, a dead person's spirit lingers for seven days until he is satisfied that his family has properly mourned and made offerings. The ghosts that are most feared are those who are hungry, whose graves have been neglected or who have died violently or far from home. In Mandarin, the word for ghost, "gui," sounds like the verb "to go home;" thus, a wandering ghost is one who is homeless.

Ah-de is also haunted by memories of his young son who died in an accident years earlier and by the wordless visits of his estranged wife. His life is drained of meaning; when he's not driving his taxi on rain-soaked highways, he practices the calligraphy for his own epitaph. His existential despair is a sort of living death, until his encounter with Mah-le inspires him to take action and to value his life again.

Ah-de personifies Taiwan's ambivalence about its political situation, a topic so sensitive it can only be treated allegorically. To do nothing—by maintaining the status quo—is to die a slow death. To take action—by voting for change, even if it's risky—is the only way out of this perpetual limbo, the only way to return the wandering ghost to his grave. There is no easy resolution here, only the certainty of stagnation if a society's collective hopes are never allowed to be expressed.

*

March 17, 2000. I spend hours surfing the websites of the BBC, CNN, the *New York Times,* and the *Taipei Times* for last-minute election news. The *Taipei Times* reported that 100,000 people attended a rally in Taipei for KMT candidate Lien Chan, while more than 400,000 supporters packed into a sports stadium in his hometown of Tainan to cheer opposition candidate Chen Shui-bian. I could spend the whole night searching for news online, but Jun and Cara invite me over for dinner, providing a welcome distraction. When I get home at midnight, I collapse on the sofa, dizzy from an excess of wine and speculation. The polls are closed by now; I cast my vote in the *Tribune*.

The dream I have is astonishing in its clarity, and I feel as though I'm waking up in a changed world. I lie in bed and replay it again and again: I am standing in a field with mountains behind me, looking at a brilliant sunset. I see a castle in the clouds, a small city actually, with trees and houses and streetlamps. I feel a profound sense of peace and happiness, but it seems too good to be true. My instinct tells me to find someone else, another pair of eyes to confirm what I've seen. A woman from my past appears—a former journalist and news anchor. I ask her: *Do you see what I see?* She nods and says yes. I rush to tell my parents the good news—that I have seen a sovereign Taiwan. They smile knowingly and say: *We were expecting it all along.*

Postscript

On March 18, 2000, the people of Taiwan elected Chen Shui-bian as their next president, ending over fifty years of Kuomintang rule and ushering in a new era for Taiwan's democracy.

Seasons of Scrabble and Mahjong

Every spring my neighborhood is full of flowering trees. I used to assume they were all cherry blossoms until I learned the differences between their delicate pink petals, the white or pink plum blossoms that cover the sidewalk in confetti, and the large, lotus-like magnolias with their creamy petals. Flowering trees remind me of my mom; she loved flowers and plants and could always identify them no matter what landscape we were in—Princeton, Taipei, Berkeley, even Paris. We would be taking a walk, and she would say *Look Gracie, that's a plum tree,* and I would look and immediately forget because I was focused on something else— what work I needed to do, where we were going to have dinner, other trivial things. Now, of course, I wish I had paid attention. I wish I had taken the time to learn more from my mom, like how to identify trees, or how to cook Taiwanese food, or the best way to tie a silk scarf. Now these things matter to me because my mother is far away, and my mother is sick.

1. BAMBOO: Summer 1998

The summer I spent three months in Taipei with my parents, the air conditioner in the living room broke in the middle of a heat wave. Though we lived in a house on top of Yangmingshan, in a cool, green, relatively unpolluted part of the city, the air felt thick and greasy, like a hot kitchen. The humidity was so high that our bath towels never completely dried, giving off a faintly sour smell. Even after the sun went down, it was still over ninety degrees inside the house. "It's like having a fever, you know," my mom said, inviting me to sleep in their bedroom for the night because their air conditioner was the only one that worked.

I remember lying on my stomach on a fold-out foam mattress on the floor in my parents' bedroom, writing in my journal and watching my mom pack for her trip to Switzerland. She was one of Taiwan's delegates to a conference of the World Council of Presbyterian Churches, and she would be gone for three and a half weeks. She selected several short-sleeved dresses from the closet—white with black roses, multicolored floral, a navy William Morris print—and carefully rolled them up, one by one, to pack into the hard-sided Samsonite that lay open like a giant blue clam on the double bed. She folded an armful of white cotton briefs into neat squares and used wads of pantyhose to fill in the odd-shaped cavities around her two pairs of pumps. She moved back and forth from the bed to the closet, energetic and purposeful in her batik nightgown and cloth slippers.

My dad sat hunched over a small desk on one side of the bedroom, squinting at handwritten notes on lined paper under the light of a fluorescent lamp. Like me, he prefers to write with ink and covers the page with messy cross-outs and marginalia when editing. His silver-white hair was damp; though he had just gotten out of the shower, I could tell from the way his undershirt stuck to him that he was already sweating again. He was revising a speech he was to give the next day for a meeting of the Taiwan Bible Society, the local branch of the international nonprofit where he had worked as a Bible translator for more than twenty-five years. In different ways, both of my parents carried on the Christian faith that their parents, grandparents, and great-grandparents had learned from nineteenth-century Western missionaries.

I wrote in my journal: *Mom is packing, and Dad is writing, all at the last minute. I come from a family of procrastinators. . . . I'm glad she's taking this trip, but why did it have to be in the middle of my trip? I'm spending three months here, which I've never done before, and she'll be gone for a third of it.*

My mom, a professor of feminist theology and Christian art at Taiwan Theological Seminary, complained about how she hadn't finished grading her papers from the spring semester and would have to do them after she finished packing. It was almost 11:00 p.m.

"You shouldn't stay up so late every night," my dad said from the other side of the room.

"I can't help it, I have no choice," she snapped back, zipping up a small cosmetic bag.

"But you've known for a month that this trip was coming up."

"*Aiyah* . . . Why are you blaming me? Don't you know I have been working so hard?" My mom sighed and squeezed her eyes shut, sinking down onto the bamboo-patterned bedspread.

"I don't need any more pressure," she whined irritably. She seemed more relaxed when she was in motion; sitting still on the edge of the bed, my mom looked tense and unhappy.

I stiffened on my makeshift bed. I wasn't used to hearing my parents fight; when they did it was usually in Taiwanese. I wondered if they were speaking English only because I was there. I felt sorry for my mom, knowing how hard she'd been working. Her career was in full bloom and her accomplishments multiplied, but I saw my dad's side too—her heavy workload was taking a toll on her health, and she seemed increasingly delicate. I wrote: *Maybe I'm part of the problem since I've taken over my mom's old office, and since Mom and Dad are taking me out all the*

time, playing Scrabble with me, and helping me with the documen-
tary. This is the first time I've lived with them since high school,
and even though I know they're happy I'm here, it's an adjustment
to have me around.

My dad had taken me aside a few days before, saying he was
worried because Mom was having trouble getting things done.
She often stayed up until 2:00 a.m. grading papers, and when he
asked her why it was taking so long, she said she had a hard time
concentrating.

"Mom, can I help you?" I asked from the floor.

"No," she said softly, "just go to bed."

It was late, but I was wide awake, so I kept writing. *Last night*
we stayed up late and I videotaped and took notes while Mom
went over the whole family tree with me. She took me through
all the kinship names—the way I'm supposed to address my rela-
tives depending on how we're related. Jī-peh means Number Two
Uncle Older Than Dad; Gō·-chím means Wife of Number Five Uncle
Younger Than Dad. It's an amazing system—compact and effi-
cient. But then again, you can go through your whole life never
knowing your elder relatives' given names.

Dad was hunched over the desk again marking up his papers
since there was nothing he could do to help her get ready. Mom
counted out Taiwan dollars, US dollars, and traveler's checks,
which she kept in separate billfolds. I wrote until my eyelids
got droopy and my handwriting became illegible. I tucked the
journal under my pillow, pulled the sheet up to my chin, and fell
asleep to the whirring of the air conditioner.

2. PLUM BLOSSOM: Winter 2000

At eight o'clock in the morning on day three of long nian, the
Year of the Dragon, I finally emerged from my twenty-four-hour

ordeal at the airport into the chilly, smoggy Taipei air. It was overcast and colder than I expected: I'd never visited before in February. My parents were bundled up in knee-length overcoats, wool scarves, and gloves. I hardly recognized them in winter clothes. Even with their bulky garments, my parents seemed smaller than I remembered; their footsteps were slower and lighter, their presence less solid.

They no longer lived at Yangmingshan, having bought an apartment in Sanhsia, where my dad had been raised and where his eldest sister, Tōa-ko· (Number One Aunt), lived. We went back to the apartment just long enough for me to unload my luggage, brush my teeth, and change my clothes before taking a taxi to meet Saⁿ-kū (Third Uncle) and his family in Tianmu, a neighborhood on the north side of Taipei. Saⁿ-kū is my mom's youngest brother, who had been seriously injured in a motorcycle accident in the 1980s and was paralyzed from the neck down. Though physically incapacitated, he is mentally sharp—he's the most talkative and opinionated of my mom's brothers, and he loves to laugh and debate. His wife, whom I call Aunt Emi, is sturdy and cheerful; she takes care of my uncle and is the only one strong enough to lift him into and out of his wheelchair. Soon after we got to their apartment, we loaded into Aunt Emi's old Toyota for the drive up to Keelung, where we would meet Jī-kū (Second Uncle) and his family to celebrate Jī-kū's birthday.

I sat between my mom and dad in the backseat and looked out the window at the mountainous landscape. The outskirts of Taipei are lush with vegetation in the summer, but this time of year all that was visible were naked trees, sprawling cemeteries with tombstones like scattered tiles, and clusters of gray cement buildings that looked like dirty teeth lining the highway.

Jī-kū and his family were already at the restaurant, a multi-floor establishment across from the harbor that specialized in seafood banquets. We sat around a large round table in a private room and toasted Jī-kū's sixtieth birthday with glasses of guava juice and whiskey. He'd aged since the last time I saw him a few years ago; his hair was mostly gray, and his dark skin was deeply creased from his cigarette habit, though he was still handsome. His wife, whose pale unlined face contrasted with her husband's, was a quiet, smiling presence by his side. Jī-kū told us that their son had just finished his military service and would come home in a few days, and we raised our glasses again.

My mom was happy to see her brothers, though she could no longer drink beer with them since she had been diagnosed with diabetes. They laughed and gossiped and asked for her advice on everything. She seemed more at ease, more accustomed to being the center of attention, than when she was with my dad's relatives. In my dad's family, she is simply Wife of Third Uncle, which has no special status, though she's treated well because my dad is the favorite brother and uncle. But in her family, she's Eldest Sister and Number One Aunt, so she is treated with deference. Her teacup never sat empty for long, and she was invited to help herself first whenever a new dish arrived.

As usual, at a table full of Taiwanese relatives, most of the conversation carried on without me. With few exceptions, none of my relatives speak more than a few words of English, and my Taiwanese was limited to domestic phrases like "let's go" and "I'm hungry." I smiled a lot and said very little. Sometimes, when there was a big burst of laughter, I would ask my mom or dad to translate. That time they were laughing about a bizarre translation of a foreign concept. Saⁿ-kū explained that my cousin was enrolled in correspondence school, but that in Mandarin the literal translation is "air college."

After lunch, Aunt Emi drove us back to Tianmu and invited us to play mahjong. She brought out the card table and handed me a small box of pushpins to attach a thin blanket to the table so we wouldn't make too much noise. We dumped out the heavy plastic mahjong tiles and mixed them up by spreading them out in a circular motion called "swimming on the table." Then we constructed four walls with the tiles face-down, each wall eighteen tiles across and two tiles high. We each rolled the dice to see who would be east wind, or the dealer for the first round. I knew that east came first, but after that I tended to lose track. When I played mahjong with my parents and brother, my mom was the one who kept track of all the complicated rules—which wind it was, whose turn it was to roll the dice, whether to play clockwise or counterclockwise, and how to score a winning hand. She was the only one who knew how.

Through years of playing mahjong, my family members all developed distinct game-playing personalities. My mom is a clever strategist; she never gives away what she's going to do. My older brother, Ted, is an excellent player too, but unlike my mom, he can't keep a poker face. He's the gambler in the family, the one most likely to take big risks for a bigger score. My dad is the least competitive among us—he's willing to play but unambitious since my mom and my brother are so good. I love it when my dad wins because he never expects it, and he becomes giddy as a child. I mostly take after my mom; I try to play quietly and conceal my advantages.

I'm a reasonably good player, but what I'm most proud of is this: Mahjong is the only social activity in which I can get by entirely in Taiwanese. Within those four walls, I'm as fluent as everyone else in the vocabulary of suits and numbers, winds and dragons. Worries about the language barrier and cultural differences dissolve as I lose myself in the game. In mahjong, I'm just another player like everyone else, and I know exactly what to do.

The four of us took our places around the mahjong table— me, my mom, my dad, and Aunt Emi. My mom was the dealer for the east round, so she rolled the dice again to determine where to break the wall and begin picking up tiles. Aunt Emi got three flowers, or wild cards, on the first hand: chrysanthemum, orchid, and plum blossom. Along with bamboo, these plants correspond to the seasons, along with the Confucian values of uprightness, purity, longevity, and perseverance. The plum blossom is the national flower of Taiwan, representing beauty and resilience.

"*Khui hoe-tiàm* (Open a flower shop)," Aunt Emi joked. The game went quickly, and we each called out the names of the tiles we discarded: la̍k bān (six characters); saⁿ tâng (three dots); sai (west wind); pe̍h (white dragon); káu soh (nine bamboo). Just as my hand was coming together, my mom said "*kàu* (arrived)," meaning she'd won. Her winning tile was it chiáu (one bamboo), represented by a bird.

"*Chiáu-á!*" she sang, smiling at me, because "little bird" used to be one of her nicknames for me.

We played two more hands before Saⁿ-kū pointed out that we were proceeding in the wrong direction, clockwise instead of counter-clockwise.

"Are you sure?" my mom asked, looking confused. My dad and Aunt Emi shrugged.

"*Bô-iàu-kín,*" Saⁿ-kū said, laughing. Doesn't matter.

"*Aiyah* . . . I am starting to forget things," my mom said, shaking her head.

We mixed the tiles again and continued playing—this time in the right direction.

3. CHRYSANTHEMUM: Autumn 2000

At the end of the year, I visited Taiwan again. I sat with my parents around the long, low coffee table in their cramped living room, surrounded by floor-to-ceiling bookcases. A large-screen TV blared Taiwanese news and was flanked by two wide cabinets displaying my dad's collection of water buffalo sculptures and framed photos of Jenny, Shelly, and Billy—my brother's kids. Old newspapers, drink coasters, remote controls, prescription and vitamin bottles, and my dad's blood pressure monitor were pushed to one side of the coffee table to make room for the Scrabble board.

My parents had been looking forward to my visit. Among other things, it meant they had a new Scrabble opponent. I started playing when I was around twelve, but my parents had been playing a lot longer. They had a Scrabble set that was almost as old as I was. The letter tiles were smooth and nicely rounded from two and a half decades of play.

Halfway through the game, I spelled the word "quince" on a triple letter score. Forty points, not bad. I was relieved to get rid of the Q.

"Quince? What's that?" my mom asked, passing me the tiles.

"Um . . . I think it's a kind of fruit," I said sheepishly. I wasn't really sure, I just knew it was a word.

My dad nodded. He had seen the word before, but he didn't know what it was either.

"Whose turn?" she asked.

"My turn," my dad said, sighing over his letters. "I have all vowels!"

About ten minutes later my mom asked again, as if she had just noticed the word on the board. "What's quince?"

I acted as though I didn't just tell her.

This was my first visit since my mom had come down with an acute kidney infection, which had kept her in bed for a couple of weeks. She had more or less recovered and was back on her feet, but her appearance worried me. Her once-round cheeks seemed hollowed out, and her dresses and skirts hung loosely on her hips. She seemed not just thinner but shrunken overall, unexpectedly fragile. She didn't carry herself the way she used to, with the confidence of a former track and field athlete. Our silhouettes were no longer identical; her shadow was smaller now, making me feel self-conscious about having put on a few pounds. For the first time in my life, I weighed more than she did.

"How are you feeling?" I asked her, more than once.

"I'm fine. I was sick for a while . . . hmmm . . . maybe last year? But I feel much better now." She smiled reassuringly.

My dad shot me a look that said, *See what I mean?* He had told me several times that her memory was getting worse. I believed my mom when she said she was feeling better, but there was something else we were worried about: she didn't remember that it had only been two months since she was very ill.

The next day, we went to Taipei to do some shopping and visit my ninety-one-year-old grandmother, who had spent the past dozen years in a private nursing home. A-má was so delicate, her skin meltingly soft, her once-sturdy arms now weightless and brittle, her smile toothless and innocent. Yet she was incredibly strong. She had borne ten children and raised them mostly on her own as my grandfather's missionary work took him away from home for months at a time. Though A-má's health had been poor for many years, her heartbeat remained strong and steady. With nine living children and more than sixty grandchildren and great-grandchildren visiting on a regular basis, she was the envy of other residents of the nursing home.

We arrived at three o'clock, took our shoes off outside, and put on slippers before entering the visiting room. A-má was sitting in her wheelchair in her customary place, nodding off. Dad knelt in front of her, while I stood to one side. A nurse brought over a plastic stool for my dad to sit on.

Pointing to me, he said "A-bú! Look who's here—your grand-daughter. Remember her name? Gu . . . Gu . . ." He coached her to say my name. "Gu-lace-uh!" Ever since I was little, my relatives had called me by my English name instead of my Taiwanese one.

I tried to make eye contact with A-má; she aimed a blank stare in my direction. We all knew she was past the point of remembering names, but her children visited every week, and they asked her the same questions over and over. If given enough hints she would say the right thing, but I don't know if this is the same as remembering. It was more of a reflex, a word association game.

"Who am I?" my dad asked. "Which chiàng am I?" He said one syllable of the nickname A-má used to call him. She stared back without answering, but he was not discouraged. He took both of her hands and asked her again, "Which chiàng am I?"

We expected her to say "Jín-chiàng," but instead she replied, "the cute one," which was also correct. My dad is the third of six sons, and as a boy his distinguishing feature was his unusu-ally big eyes, which made him cuter than his brothers. We were impressed by A-má's improvisation.

The quiz continued. Dad asked, "Who's older, you or me?"

"You," she said.

We laughed. We'd learned not to expect too much, to be happy when A-má gave stock answers like a mechanical doll. But the occasional witty comeback reminded us that her personality was intact, though rarely visible, like a flower blooming amidst the decay.

Dad picked up a small diary that the family used to record our visits to A-má. *December 8. Jin came with Tian-hiong and Grace. A-bú is in good spirits today.* He moved to one of the side chairs and my mom took his place on the stool. She took A-má's hands and started singing Christian hymns with her. A-má wasn't lucid enough to have a conversation, but she could remember the words to a few songs, so singing was always a part of our visit.

"*Iâ-so· thià^n góa . . .*" My mom began singing the Taiwanese version of "Jesus Loves Me" and paused to make sure A-má could follow along. I didn't know the Taiwanese words, so I sang along quietly in English. Next my mom sang a children's nursery rhyme called "Ten Little Chicken Eggs." She moved in close so A-má could see her, and counted down with her fingers: *ten eggs, nine eggs, eight eggs . . .* I was happy to see her taking care of A-má, that instinct hadn't changed or diminished at all. My mom sang slightly out of tune, but in perfect tempo. I hummed along.

My dad looked lost in thought. He still had the diary open on his lap. I wondered if he was thinking, *Here are all the women in my life, and I have to take care of them all.*

Later that night, at home, my mom said, "Let's play Scrabble!" So the three of us gathered around the coffee table again. Dad and Mom both got seven-letter words, while I struggled through the game with nothing but low-point letters. I took my time adding up the final score: Mom, 188 points, Me, 142 points, Dad, 209 points.

"You won," I said to my dad.

"Haha!" He let out a little yell. My dad was genuinely surprised; he's used to losing to my mom. My mom wasn't winning as much as she used to, but that didn't dampen her enthusiasm, and she proposed another match. We dumped the letters into the box and mixed them up, then we turned the tiles over one by one until they were all face-down. We turned ourselves over to another game, another contest to see how skill and concentration could overcome accidents and chance. In Scrabble, there are no unfair advantages or disadvantages. The only difference between players is seven letters.

4. ORCHID: Spring 2002

Two years later, I was back in Taiwan for spring break. But it wasn't a leisure trip—I was there to attend A-má's funeral. My cousin Leng and I arrived on Friday night, and after picking us up from the airport, my parents took us out for a late dinner of chúi-kiáu dumplings. On Saturday, Leng's parents, Uncle I-to and Auntie Huichin, arrived in Sanhsia, and we all convened at Tōa-ko·'s house.

We gathered in their sitting room and the elder relatives talked while Leng and I munched on green tea-flavored roasted watermelon seeds. Mom asked me, "Where's Dad?" and I reminded her that he was picking up my brother Ted from the airport. Uncle I-to opened his briefcase to give Leng and me the neatly typed English translation of the program for A-má's memorial service. The entire text wasn't translated, only the names of hymns, scripture notations, and thematic headings summarizing A-má's life and service: "A Typical Gracious Mother, Assisting Husband's Career, Educating Children, Playing the Organ, Singing Hymns, Talents in Knitting and Embroidery," "Oppressed by Japanese, Escaping from the Disasters of War, Enduring Innumerable Hardships, Risking Life for Survival," "Caring for Husband Wholeheartedly in His Sickbed, Unceasing Zeal for Evangelism, Comparable to the Younger Years," and so on. The headings struck me as melodramatic, a series of movie marquees trumpeting my grandmother's extremely humble life.

Tōa-ko· got up every few minutes to refill our ceramic cups with freshly brewed oolong tea. Mom asked me again, "Where's Dad? What time is Teddy coming?" The others pretended not to notice that she was repeating herself. I told her gently that we wouldn't see them until dinnertime.

My dad told me that my mom had gotten lost in Taipei a couple of times—a city she had lived in for twenty years. She forgot where she was going and didn't recognize the street she was
on and had to take a taxi home. Ever since she'd started having
memory problems, she'd been increasingly dependent on my
dad and would fret whenever he wasn't around. The more fragile
she became, the more she leaned on him. Though it was unspoken, I knew that it was my responsibility to keep an eye on my
mom while he was away.

Ko·-tiūⁿ (Tōa-ko's husband) invited us to see the bonsai garden that my cousin Êng-iāu had carefully cultivated in the back
of the family compound where several generations of Tōa-ko·'s
family lived. Êng-iāu is their youngest son and the most finan-
cially successful member of the extended Loh clan. He owns
Sanhsia's largest and most modern dental clinic, which occupies
half of the first floor of the family compound. We went through
the sliding doors of the dental clinic—walking around hygien-
ists with paper masks, bent over silent patients—and followed
Ko·-tiūⁿ to get to the back door that led to the garage and ter-
raced garden.

Just outside the door, the gardener, a dark-skinned, soft-
spoken man, patiently tended to a hundred-year-old bonsai on
a waist-high platform. The tree was about two feet tall with a
c-shaped trunk and twenty-odd branches spreading out in an
umbrella shape. Each branch was wrapped around with bark-
colored aluminum wire—thicker at the trunk and finer near the
ends—that was designed to train the branches to grow a certain
way. The newest shoots stuck out at right angles; once trimmed
and wrapped with wire, the gardener would gently press them
into place. I hadn't known trees could be shaped so deliber-
ately. That explained why all the bonsai in Êng-iāu's garden had
branches that extended horizontally rather than upward, evenly

spaced to achieve balance and proportion. Each one was a living specimen of endless refinement, a monument to the perfection of old age.

"You can tell I'm ready to retire because I find these things interesting now," Uncle I-to joked as the gardener demonstrated the finer points of bonsai maintenance. Just then, I realized I didn't know where my mom was.

"Have you seen my mom?" I asked, scanning the backyard. Both aunties shook their heads, Uncle I-to shrugged, Leng said, "no." I tried to remember . . . We all walked out together, right? Was my mom standing here a minute ago? Before coming out, we had paused to admire some of the antiques in Êng-iāu's office inside the clinic. Did she get separated from us? Turn down a different hallway? I walked inside and retraced my steps to the courtyard, checking the clinic's restroom on the way. Empty.

The compound has two main entrances: the front gate that opens onto a big street, and the back door just below the bonsai garden. Several small streets abut the property, leading in many directions—to the temple, to the market, to my parents' apartment a few blocks away, to the next town. With so many people coming and going at any given time, it would be easy for my mom to slip out unnoticed.

I saw Ko·-tiū^n in the courtyard and asked, "Have you seen my mom?" He doesn't speak English, but I knew he understood what I was saying. He said, "no." Maybe she's in the sitting room watching TV. Maybe she never came out in the first place. I opened the screen door, strode through the dining room with the lacquered round dining table, and opened another door to look in the sitting room. She wasn't there. Did she think we were going home when we got up to see the garden? Did she go outside? I rushed back to the courtyard and stood in the front entryway, looking left and right down the street for a woman in a flowered dress and navy blazer, carrying a black purse in one hand and a dark green umbrella in the other. How far can she walk in ten minutes? Does she have her keys? I walked back through the clinic to the garden, where Leng and the others had spread out to look at the different bonsai specimens.

"I can't find my mom," I announced as I came through the door, my voice edged with anxiety.

"She's right there," Uncle I-to said, pointing up to the top of the driveway, which was partially obscured by the collection of bonsai. She had walked ahead of us and had been up there admiring the trees and flowers while we chatted with the gardener. I walked up the driveway, my heart still pounding. My mom was examining a slender fruit tree in a terracotta flowerpot next to one of Êng-iāu's cars.

"See that tree? What's the name in English?" She smiled at me.

"I was looking for you! I didn't know where you were." I sounded like a mother scolding her child.

"I was right here," she said, ignoring the worry in my voice. She pointed to the tree again. "It has a small orange fruit, but not citrus. It has a pit, like an apricot."

"I don't know. Kumquat?"

Just like that, the world shifted back to its natural order. I forgot that I was trying to change the script; I forgot my fear that I didn't know how. She was my mother again, the one who knew things, the one who was helping *me* find my way.

"No, it's something else. I'll think of it later," she said, looping her arm through mine.

Going Home

On Tuesday, October 4, 2005, my mom was reported missing from her home. I didn't find out until more than twenty-four hours later when I was in my office in San Francisco. My husband called and said, "Check your email. There's a message from your Uncle I-to. It's urgent."

He declined to tell me what the message said and insisted I read it myself. My heart plummeted. In the few seconds it took me to log into my personal email account, my mind raced with alarming scenarios familiar to anyone with ailing parents who live far away. I braced myself for bad news, wondering how I would keep my composure as the details of my parents' emergency punctured the fog of my dreary corporate day job.

I learned from Uncle I-to that my dad had been hosting a meeting of translators in his home office on the ninth floor, a separate unit in the same high-rise apartment complex as my parents' residence (the fourth floor) in Sanhsia. They were discussing the progress on a new Taiwanese translation of the Bible, a multiyear project that would be my dad's swan song—the crowning achievement of more than three decades as a translator. Although he was officially retired from the United Bible Societies, where he'd worked ever since I was two years old, my dad remains the senior consultant and most esteemed member of the six-person translation team.

My mom had been in the room with the translation committee since my dad could no longer leave her unsupervised due to her worsening dementia. The doctor diagnosed Alzheimer's in 2000, the year both my parents turned sixty-five and were supposed to begin enjoying their retirement. There was nothing we could do except watch my mom become less and less articulate and increasingly confused, disconnected, and dependent, until she could no longer tell what time it was, what day it was, or whether she had eaten five minutes or five hours ago.

Memory loss is the most salient feature of Alzheimer's. We didn't realize until later that we would be contending with a constellation of behavioral problems such as stubbornness, hostility, mood swings, and paranoia. After forty years of companionable marriage, my mom became angry, resentful, and suspicious of my dad, who in her eyes was no longer a caring, devoted husband but a dominating, larger-than-life force in her steadily diminishing universe.

That afternoon, as the meeting carried on without her, my mom became restless and upset. She decided she'd had enough of these "rude people" who were excluding her from the conversation and announced around four o'clock that she wanted to go home.

My dad—mindful of the committee that had traveled an hour out of the city to meet with him, since he was no longer free to attend long meetings in Taipei—didn't follow my mom as she stepped out. She rarely went anywhere unchaperoned, but he did not want her constant interruptions to interfere with the group's work. He thought my mom would either go across the courtyard to the fourth-floor apartment or go down the street to Tōa-ko·'s house. He continued the meeting.

A while later, he called the apartment to check on her, but there was no answer. Next he called Tōa-ko· to see if my mom had gone to her house, but she wasn't there either. My dad apologized to his colleagues and ended the meeting, then he walked the ten minutes to Tōa-ko·'s house, searching up and down the street as he went. By then it was past five o'clock; she had been gone for an hour.

"Wandering" is the name given to the tendency of Alzheimer's patients to walk away from familiar surroundings and quickly get lost. For someone with dementia, what might seem like a harmless excursion can become a life-threatening situation. It's estimated that a person with Alzheimer's who wanders away and isn't found within twenty-four hours has only a 50 percent chance of surviving.

No one had any idea where my mom went. She seldom ventured anywhere and often didn't enjoy being out for more than a short period of time before complaining that she was tired and wanted to go home. She lost interest in activities she once enjoyed, like going to bookstores, museums, and her favorite department stores. No matter where they were—at the local vegetable market, in Taipei at the doctor's office, or attending a large family gathering—my dad would cut short whatever they were doing, make polite excuses if needed, and take my mom home.

He never believed he was doing anything but accommodating her wishes. So whenever she whined, "I want to go home" when they actually *were* at home, my dad was bewildered. "We *are* home," he would insist. But my mom would put on her jacket and make for the door with a sense of urgency he could never understand. "Where are you going?" "I want to go home!" She'd howl as though he was detaining her against her will.

One of the things I've always admired about my parents is they truly had a marriage of equals. They both earned PhDs, were successful and respected in their fields, and performed an equal share of domestic duties. They were a couple that other couples envied. After forty years of marriage, I don't think they were prepared for how the disease would test their relationship, leading to a power struggle that was hopelessly lopsided. Out of necessity and love, my dad went from being my mom's companion to being her guardian, a controlling presence in her life. The more her health declined, the more she needed him. But she resisted it, too, and I know she felt the loss of her independence deeply.

It was a little after five o'clock when my dad and Tōa-ko· arrived at the police station to file a missing person report. My dad calmly described his wife's appearance: seventy years old, five feet two inches tall, slender, short black hair that was permed and going gray at the roots, wire-rimmed glasses, dressed in a floral-print housedress and high-heeled shoes. He explained that she had dementia and was confused and disoriented. I'm sure he was calm and stoic as usual, his steady voice concealing his mounting panic. The officer nodded and took notes.

The last time I had seen my mom was a year and a half earlier when my husband and I visited Taiwan six months after our wedding. At times she seemed confused by the change in her daily routine since we were constantly going out, but she was otherwise relaxed and easygoing. My conversations with her tended to come back to the same topics over and over, as though she was trying to reassure herself that she knew the basic facts of my life: *You live in San Francisco? In California? Are you in school? Oh, you graduated! I didn't know. You are working now?*

By then I was used to the repetitive questions and more amused than alarmed by her non sequiturs. She remembered my husband, Anil, and she remembered we were married, so I convinced myself she was doing okay. My dad would take me aside and say, "She's getting worse," and would tell me about how irritable she was and how she had occasional delusions, like when she insisted she was late to an important meeting. He'd correct her and say that no one was waiting for her, which would make her even more upset. I told him, "Dad, there's no point in fighting over it. Just go along with it and agree with her once in a while. There's no harm in it. If you correct her all the time, you'll just hurt her feelings."

We had this same conversation on the telephone, numerous times, in the months following that visit. Even though my dad tried to describe the ways in which my mom continued to decline, to me it sounded like the status quo. I could not see first-hand what was happening to her, and the months stretched to more than a year. I wanted to visit, but there was always something holding me back. *My job's not flexible . . . I might be pregnant . . . We're thinking of moving . . . We can't spend the money right now.*

I didn't want to admit it, but I felt stifled by the new contours of my life. After finishing my MFA in creative writing, I was burned out and willingly put my writing on hold. I planned my wedding, got a full-time job, and channeled my energy into learning how to be a wife and an employee at a large corporation. But as time went by, I felt increasingly guilty about abandoning my creative life. Even though I set aside a few hours each weekend to write, I found it difficult to peel back all the layers to reach the state of heightened contemplation that I needed to write from my heart. I felt like I needed to travel away from myself in order to find the self that could write again. As much as I wanted to make the journey, I resisted it at the same time. Writing about what matters to me, about my family and my history, required a level of solitude and spaciousness that I no longer had and wasn't sure I could ever get back.

What I couldn't see at the time was that just as my parents' relationship was being tested by my mom's dementia, my own marriage was being tested in its own way. Unlike me, my parents had four decades of marriage behind them with many shared dreams and trials. They had learned how to compromise and negotiate, to accept the good and the bad in what was to be a lifelong union.

Meanwhile, I was still taking the first wobbly steps in my own marriage. My husband and I were both fiercely independent, having lived far away from our families for more than a decade. After years of each being on our own, we were thrilled to find each other. It was a relief to have someone to depend on and come home to, someone who'd open a bottle of wine to celebrate good news or run to the store for medicine if I had a fever. On the other hand, I was not used to being tethered, to being responsible for another person who in turn was responsible for me. Living in a different country from our families had given each of us a kind of freedom that wasn't easy to give up. We were still learning to be vulnerable, to let the other person in, to give and ask for help in a way that didn't come naturally.

A year into our relationship, we had our first big fight. I had given up my one-bedroom apartment in a chic neighborhood of San Francisco to move into Anil's spacious two-bedroom in North Oakland, next to a golf course. I sold or gave away most of my furniture, and we bought a few things to fill the gaps in our new, joint household. He had strong preferences when it came to décor, favoring dark wood furniture and linear patterns. For the most part I thought he had good taste.

One day we went shopping at Bed Bath & Beyond. Our cart was loaded with small appliances, new bath towels, and various other knickknacks to satisfy our domestic yearnings. I selected a new comforter set in a muted gray-violet with a wavy stripe and floral pattern. It seemed like the perfect compromise between his preference for dark, masculine colors and my softer, more natural style. I showed it to him and was surprised when he scowled at me.

"Did you even look at the price tag? This is way overpriced!"

"But I don't like any of the other designs. This one will go perfectly with everything else in the bedroom."

"We are not spending that kind of money on bedding. No way."

We stared at each other for a long moment. He was right; the comforter set was nearly twice as much as some of the others. He pulled out other options for me to look at. "What about this one? This one?"

Normally I am very receptive to other people's suggestions. I hate conflict; I'm usually the first to compromise. So even I was surprised by how I reacted next.

"Why can't I have this *one* thing? Everything we have now is something *you* chose, reflecting *your* taste. There's nothing that reflects me at all!"

I stood there fighting back tears until he finally relented. He was embarrassed by my meltdown but also astonished at how insistently I fought back. It wasn't just about the comforter. Even though I usually went along with his decisions, I did not want this to be taken for granted; I was not ready to let someone else make all my choices for me. And yet, the act of getting married was exactly that—a pledge that I would trust someone to act in my best interests if, one day, I could no longer do that for myself. My mom's dementia was the first real crisis we faced as a married couple, and one that forced us to confront the reality of marriage after the scripted perfection of our wedding day, after the honeymoon was over and the wedding gifts were put away. We were witnessing what it really means to love and commit to someone for better or for worse, in sickness and in health.

One night, when I was working late in my office, I had a conversation with the cleaning lady, Maria. I saw her a few times a week when she would come to empty out the trash bins in our cubicles. She was a sweet, older Latina woman who always greeted me and seemed to appreciate our brief interactions.

That evening, she asked me what I had done for Mother's Day the previous Sunday.

"Nothing," I said.

"Oh," she sighed. "You don't have kids?" She looked concerned.

"No, not yet."

Her face brightened again. "Did you see your mother?"

"No, she lives in Taiwan, but I talked to her on the phone."

Her face crumpled. "That is too bad! You have no kids, and your mother is so far away!"

For a moment I didn't know what to say.

"Well, I hope you see your mother soon!" she said as she wheeled away her cleaning cart, and I turned back to my desk and blinked away tears.

I thought about my parents from time to time and wondered how they were doing. I kept reminding myself to call them more often, but I was always too tired or preoccupied, or it was too late, or I wasn't in the mood. Days would go by, sometimes weeks, before I could bring myself to make the call. When I did, the conversations were brief and predictable. My dad would tell me that my mom was getting worse, that she was being difficult, that she was having delusions, that she sometimes refused to eat, and that the medication didn't seem to do much for her. He could not elaborate because my mom was within earshot and would get upset that he was talking about her. To try and avert this, he would put my mom on the phone, and we'd have the following conversation:

"Hi, Mom!"

"Hi, Gracie!"

"How are you?"

"I'm fine! Thank you." (She said this no matter how she was feeling.)

"Did you go to church today?"

"Church . . . ? I don't know. Let me ask Daddy."

"Never mind, Mom. That's okay."

"Where are you? You live in . . . ah . . . ?"

"Oakland, near San Francisco. You came here for my wedding, remember?"

"I did? Oh. That's right."

My mom would reach her conversational limit within a minute or two and put my dad back on the phone. After spending all of our time talking about my mom, I'd ask him:

"So how are *you*?"

He'd pause. "Well . . . I'm surviving."

"Dad, I thought you were going to hire a housekeeper. You can't do everything by yourself. You need a break."

"We'll see. Auntie Tōa-ko· is going to check with the agency for me."

"How's your health?"

Another pause. "Okay. The same . . . I better go now! Mom is getting impatient. Thank you for calling!"

I'd go to bed thinking about the weariness in my dad's voice and feeling like my heart was going to break from all the things that were left unsaid. I'd feel guilty about not doing more and helpless for being so far away. *I would visit if I could.*

And then I'd wake up the next morning and go back to life as usual.

I could not begin to perceive how things were changing for my parents until I received that email from Uncle I-to. In an instant, I was forced to see that the shifts in my mom's behavior and mood were not benign at all. She was now a threat to her own safety; she had crossed over into new territory that none of us, including my dad, were equipped to deal with.

While my dad was at the police station reporting my mom missing, the telephone rang. The officer picked up the phone and started taking notes. "Where? What does she look like? Hold on." Someone had called the station to say he saw a woman walking by herself along a deserted mountain road and she appeared to be hurt. She matched my mom's description. Another officer was sent to drive to where the woman had been seen, and he took my dad with him.

They drove up toward the mountains, along a wooded country road where there were few cars or people. Despite having grown up in Sanhsia, my dad didn't know where the road led. It was twenty minutes before they stopped, at least five or six miles away from the center of town. My dad said he and the officer got out of the car and saw my mom sitting on the ground surrounded by a group of farmers. She was bleeding from her jaw and ear, her clothes were wet, and her pantyhose were torn. They guessed she had fallen into a creek along the road and injured herself. She was not wearing her glasses, but they were found in her purse, along with some tissues, an empty coin purse, and a clean pair of underwear.

My dad didn't ask a lot of questions when they found her; he was just relieved that my mom was safe. The officer drove my parents to the hospital in Sanhsia, where my mom was diagnosed with a "mandible fracture" and sent for immediate observation to National Taiwan University Hospital in Taipei. They stayed there overnight.

He didn't contact me right away because he was with my

mom at the hospital. I wasn't able to reach him by phone until a day after it happened. I learned the facts from my uncle's email, and he apologized for being the bearer of bad news and suggested that I call my parents more often.

I was ashamed that I was not doing more to help my parents. Although they never questioned my decision to stay in California after graduating from the University of California at Berkeley, at times like this I wondered if I was a bad daughter for not living closer to them. In a way it wasn't my choice to make; I grew up American and barely spoke any Taiwanese or Mandarin. I would never be able to live comfortably in Taiwan. Even if I did possess the language and social skills to do it, I had just made several major life decisions—getting married, signing a lease on an apartment, and getting a full-time job—that tied me more firmly than ever to California.

"I have to go to Taiwan," I told my husband. The timing was terrible. Things were not going well at my job; my boss made me the scapegoat for problems in our department, and I was convinced that she was trying to get me to quit. While I desperately wanted to leave, our financial situation and the need for health benefits required me to stay. Asking for a leave of absence—which I needed to do since I had used up my vacation time—would put me even more at risk. Anil was in the middle of interviewing for jobs after taking a year off to write a book. We both knew the importance of being available to talk to recruiters as soon as they showed interest; being away for any length of time would slow down his momentum.

On top of that, we had just moved into a new apartment the day before I received the email from Uncle I-to. This was our first big project as a married couple—finding a suitable place that was neither mine nor his but was truly *ours* and would give us room to grow and eventually start a family. We were eating off paper plates and sleeping on mismatched sheets as we slowly unpacked one box after another. Our struggle to recreate a functional household was like putting together a giant three-dimensional puzzle with millions of pieces. The boxes were just the start; we still had furniture and supplies to buy, change of address forms to fill out, phone calls to make, and new routines to establish. We hadn't even had a chance to get our bearings in the new apartment yet.

Our lives were in disarray. At a time when we needed to focus on building and cementing our ties to each other, we had to drop everything to contend with my parents' situation. My husband was unhappy about the disruption—we both were—but I was too overwhelmed with my own stress and grief to empathize with his frustration. I felt I had no choice; nothing was going to keep me away from my parents when they needed me.

It had been a year and a half since I last saw them, and I was not prepared for how much things had deteriorated and how vulnerable they had become. I finally had to face what my dad had been trying to tell me for so many months: that my mom was slipping away. I felt an encompassing sadness at this loss, but also, hidden beneath it, a feeling I couldn't quite name. Looking back, I now see the shadow for what it was: anger at having to choose between a life with my parents in Taiwan and a life of my own in California. I could not have both. We were not like other families who lived their entire lives in close proximity. Once I graduated from high school, we never again lived in the same country. We were always half a world apart.

The soonest we could visit Taiwan was two weeks after the incident. I called my dad every other day to check on how my mom was doing. Her jaw and ear were bandaged up, and she complained that her side hurt. She was very tired for several days and didn't try to walk out on her own. She did not seem to remember getting lost. When I talked to her on the phone and asked her how she was, she said what she always said: "I'm fine! Thank you." Even as her conversational skills declined and she spoke English less and less, that reflex never failed.

The days leading up to the trip were a blur. I went to my job and acted as normal as I could, but I had a pit in my stomach that would not go away. I was haunted by the fact that I was going back to a mother who might be unrecognizable to me.

The image that I had of her—of an accomplished and dignified woman whose intellectual and social skills were gradually fading—was replaced by a more disturbing picture: a lonely, gaunt figure walking uphill on an unpaved road as it's getting dark outside, undeterred by the dirt and pebbles that are ruining her nice shoes. She is not worried about who or what she might encounter on this desolate path; she hurries toward some unseen destination that remains just out of reach, yet she is convinced that she is almost there. She has been walking for more than an hour, ignoring the pain in her feet, unaware of how many miles she has covered. She trips and falls into a creek, soaking her dress and cutting her face on a rock. She almost loses her glasses, but that doesn't stop her. Stumbling, bleeding, disheveled, it doesn't matter . . . She is determined to go to that place that only she knows.

I want to go home.

Vortex

We arrived on a Saturday in mid-October. Anil and I stayed in the spare bedroom of my parents' ninth floor apartment. My aunt who lives in Tamsui, Tōa-ḿ, had referred my dad to a nonprofit foundation that provides temporary caregivers to families in transition. She arranged for the foundation director and caregiver to visit us on Tuesday morning. Anil stayed in the bedroom while I went out to join the meeting with my dad, mom, aunt, caregiver, and the foundation director.

The foundation director was a slight, middle-aged man with glasses and a confident manner. Armed with a thick folder of brochures and documentation, he spoke about his organization and explained the services offered. The caregiver, Miss Bai, was a woman a little older than me with a round face, sturdy build, and loud voice—rather matronly, like an English governess, except she was Taiwanese. She spoke a little bit about her experience as a caregiver and said that she had cared for her elderly mother who had Alzheimer's. She knew some Taiwanese but defaulted to speaking Mandarin.

I did not understand most of what they talked about, but I felt it was important to be there. I occupied myself by pouring tea for everyone and setting out snacks. Out of the corner of my eye, I noticed a tiny ant crawling on the plate of cashews, so I discreetly took it back into the kitchen and threw the nuts away. Then I went back to the living room and sat next to my mom on the loveseat. She was quiet through most of the meeting; she and I were present for the discussion, yet we remained somehow apart. I couldn't tell if she was listening to the others, but she must have been aware that they were talking about her.

At one point my mom turned to me and said calmly, "You know, dying is fine." My heart leapt to my throat. My dad and aunt were deep in conversation with the foundation director, and I don't think they heard her. She sounded completely genuine, as though she was trying to reassure me with some timeless wisdom. But we had never previously discussed any of the big questions about life or death; I did not have those kinds of conversations with my parents.

I stared at my mom in disbelief, and even now I still don't know whether she was experiencing a moment of extraordinary lucidity and telling me not to be afraid or whether she was babbling incoherently and losing her grasp of English, her mouth forming around sounds whose meaning she no longer quite understood. The conversation continued around us; I didn't know what to do except nod silently in acknowledgment, trying to swallow the lump in my throat.

My dad signed the contract for one month of caregiver visits from Miss Bai. It included general housekeeping, cooking, and care of my mom for eight hours a day, six days a week, with a one-hour rest break and an allowance for transportation from the next town. She would start the next day.

It was around one o'clock when we thanked Miss Bai and the foundation director and showed them out. I fetched Anil from the bedroom, and we all went out for lunch. My dad said he knew a vegetarian restaurant that was across the Sanhsia River on the other side of the bridge, about a twenty-minute walk from the apartment.

My dad walked arm-in-arm with my mom, my aunt walked in the middle, and Anil and I walked behind them. We passed through the center of town, inhaling the scent of incense as we crossed the plaza in front of Qingshui Zushi Temple and made our way to the bridge. We walked underneath the ornate Chinese arches and past several sculptures of stone lions. While the bridge itself is quite attractive, the river below is partially dried up and filled with swampy weeds.

On weekends and festival days, the bridge is usually crowded with street vendors selling sweets, clothes, toys, and trinkets. Sometimes there would be a man singing folk songs accompanied by a high-pitched string instrument, or groups of boys using long ropes to spin colorful wooden tops shaped like inverted Hershey's Kisses. That day the bridge was mostly empty of commerce except for a couple of lonely merchants selling small jade or metal figurines of Buddhas and zodiac animals spread out on a blanket. Although the displays were not very impressive, my dad would always pause to see if there were any water buffalos to add to his collection.

"So, what happened during the meeting?" Anil asked me.

"We met the caregiver from the foundation, and she seems quite nice," I told him. "She has experience with Alzheimer's. My dad hired her on the spot, and she'll start working tomorrow."

"That's good. What did your mom say?"

I took a deep breath. "She didn't say much, she just sat there quietly." I couldn't bring myself to repeat what she had said to me. The blood rushed to my face, but I pushed back my emotions. *Not now, not here.* I didn't want to start crying in front of everyone.

Once we reached the other side of the bridge, we turned

down one of the major roads to get to the restaurant. But after walking several blocks without seeing a sign for a vegetarian restaurant, my dad told us to turn around.

"I thought it was here . . . But maybe it was on the other street."

My dad said it had been more than a year since he went to the restaurant, and he didn't remember the exact location. It was almost two o'clock and we were hungry and impatient. Finally my dad stopped a woman on the street to ask if she knew where the vegetarian restaurant was. The woman pointed to a restaurant we had already walked past and said that it used to be there, but it closed a few months ago. It was now a shabu-shabu (hot-pot) restaurant.

Anil muttered under his breath, "You mean we walked all that way just to have shabu-shabu again?"

I sighed. "We'll eat better tomorrow, okay?" I was tired of apologizing for the limited food options in Sanhsia; my parents didn't cook anymore since my mom's condition had worsened. We frequently ate at a shabu-shabu restaurant near the apartment because it was one of the few places we could enjoy a meal that didn't have meat in it. We had walked almost a mile by then, which was not a big deal for Anil and me but was beyond my dad's usual level of exertion since he was in the early stages of Parkinson's and was easily fatigued.

The restaurant was slightly run down and almost empty. I was grateful that my aunt was with us; she was animated and chatty and pretended that the food was good for our sake, since the lunch was meant to be a gesture of thanks for her role in setting up the meeting. Although she is well over sixty, a widow, and a grandmother of four, she still has an infectious smile and a twinkle in her eye that make her seem much younger than her years.

On our way out, I told Anil, "Why don't you walk with my dad, and I'll walk with my mom and my aunt."

I knew he wanted a chance to speak candidly with my dad. We knew we'd eventually have to broach the delicate topic of estate planning. It was hard to have serious conversations at the apartment; my mom didn't like it when people talked about her, so we'd have to go into another room to discuss things. It wouldn't take long for her to notice that we were doing something without her, and she'd come looking for us. We'd have to change the topic or join her in the other room to avoid arousing suspicion. At some point we realized that the only time we could really talk to my dad about my mom's condition was when we were walking outside. Because Sanhsia's streets are so narrow and there are no sidewalks, only two people can walk side-by-side at the edge of the road. The street noise makes it almost impossible to overhear anyone, so it was the perfect way for all of us to be together while having separate and private conversations.

On the way home, my dad got a call on his cell phone. A few months earlier, Tōa-ko· had helped him make arrangements to hire a full-time, live-in housekeeper from an agency that recruits domestic workers from overseas. Tōa-ko· had hired an Indonesian housekeeper through this agency and recommended that my dad do the same so that he would have some assistance with basic cleaning, shopping, and cooking. Because the workers came from overseas, they needed to obtain work visas, and it usually took several months for the process to go through.

The call was from the agency—apparently the visa application had been completed and the housekeeper was going to arrive in Taiwan the very next day. This was a surprise—the last time my dad had communicated with the agency, all they could say was that the application was being processed. They had no idea how long it would take. Now, all of a sudden, he was expected to be ready for a live-in housekeeper to arrive within twenty-four hours. She was already under contract to my dad, so he would be responsible for her from the minute she landed in Taipei.

The timing was awkward. Not only had he not received advance warning of this development, but my dad had literally just signed a contract for Miss Bai to provide housekeeping and caregiving services for one month, also beginning the next day. I doubt that he would have taken that step if he had known that the arrival of the live-in housekeeper was imminent.

My dad told us the news after he hung up the phone, and immediately we began discussing what needed to be done to get ready for the housekeeper's arrival. The young woman's name was Herlina—like many Indonesians, she did not have a sur-name. She was twenty-two years old and knew a little bit of Eng-lish and a little bit of Mandarin, but not much. This was her first assignment, so she would have to be trained from scratch. My aunt suggested that the two helpers could work in tandem—Miss Bai, being more experienced, could train and mentor Herlina. My dad agreed that that was a good idea.

While these were both positive developments, my dad must have felt overwhelmed that it was all happening at once. With less than a day's notice he had to prepare for someone he'd never met to move into the fourth-floor apartment with him and my mom.

"Grace, can you help me clean out Mommy's office? I think Herlina will sleep there."

"Sure," I said.

"I'm going to have to spend a few hours over there," I told Anil.

He nodded wearily.

"You know, I don't think we can go to Taipei tomorrow. There's too much going on. I want to be here when Miss Bai and Herlina start working. I think it's important for me to get to know them and help where I can."

"All right." He heaved a big sigh. I felt bad because I had been promising that we would go to Taipei soon. It was our only time to be alone and to have a little fun shopping and walking around. The day trips to Taipei were one of the few things that made our Taiwan visits enjoyable. Even though I was there to spend time with my parents and Anil came to support me, staying in Sanhsia for days at a time was claustrophobic. There wasn't much to do. Going to Taipei at least immersed us in a more interesting environment, and it relieved my dad from worrying about how to entertain us or where we would eat.

As we walked home, I could sense Anil's growing frustration. My aunt climbed in a taxi to return home to Tamsui, so it was just the four of us now, walking in formation. Anil walked ahead with my dad and tried to convince him to install new locks on the door to prevent my mom from wandering, while I walked arm in arm with my mom, attempting to make small talk. I heard snippets of their conversation.

"With all due respect Mr. Loh . . . don't you think it would be safer . . . I'm sure they could do it the same day . . ."

I heard my dad politely but firmly refuse.

We reached the lobby of the apartment building. I told my dad, "We're going back to the ninth floor to rest for a while, then I'll come over and help you clean up for Herlina."

"Okay. See you later."

As soon as we got upstairs, Anil said, "Grace, I can't take it anymore. I don't even know why I'm here. I'm just wasting my time."

He threw a few things into his roller suitcase and zipped it up, then grabbed his red backpack and made for the door.

"What are you doing? Where are you going?" I yelled.

"I'm leaving. I'm taking the next flight home. There's no point in me being here, okay?"

"Anil, stop! You're not going anywhere." I grabbed the handle of his suitcase. It was heavy and hard to maneuver, but I managed to wrest it away from him.

"Fine!" He yelled and strode out the door with the backpack over his shoulder. The elevator requires a key card, and he didn't have one, so he began running down the nine flights of stairs. I ran after him.

"Anil, come back! You can't leave now. You don't even know where you're going!"

"I can figure it out."

We were outside the building now, walking toward the main intersection where the taxis drive by. He walked fast to try and get ahead of me, and I had to run to catch up.

"Anil, please. Can we just talk?"

"Why bother? Nobody wants me here. You leave me out of most of the conversations. Your dad doesn't even like me."

"What are you talking about?"

"He won't listen to me. He just looks at me like this is none of my business."

"That's not true! He wants our help and needs our help. We just got here. You can't expect things to change overnight."

"Your dad won't listen to common sense. I'm tired of being the only one who wants to get things done around here."

Anil stuck his arm out and tried to hail a taxi, but no one stopped for him. It might have been because they were all full or because few taxi drivers in Sanhsia had the courage to pick up a scowling, six-foot-two-inch foreigner with dark skin and a shaved head. I was briefly conscious of how we must have looked—a man and a woman having a loud public argument, in English, the woman hanging on to the man's sleeve while he tries to shake her off.

Anil started walking up the main road toward the freeway.

"Where are you going? You can't leave like this. What am I going to tell my dad?"

"Who cares? I'm sure he'll be glad that I'm gone."

"That's not true! And he talks to you more openly than he does to Ted. He actually listens to you."

"That's because your brother barely contributes! Why am I, the son-in-law, doing more for your parents than their own son? Why am I the one who's getting you to discuss estate planning with your dad and spending a week and a half here while your brother skips off after forty-eight hours?"

"Okay, yes, you're more responsible than Ted, which is another reason you should stay."

"Why, when no one appreciates me here? No one has any clue how much I do for your family."

"Stop it, you know that's not true. They appreciate us both being here. Will you please come back? At least come upstairs with me, and I'll call the airline and find out whether there's a flight, okay?"

I had no intention of helping him leave, but I thought this might convince him to return to the apartment, where I could hopefully change his mind.

We had walked nearly a mile to the edge of town. It was overcast but humid, and the breeze from all the cars going by blew my hair into my face. I was starting to get a headache from the pollution.

I kept trying to reason with him. On the outside I was calm and rational, but inside I was collapsing. I was both angry and terrified of being abandoned. *How dare you act so selfishly?* I thought. *How dare you add another crisis to the one we're already in?* I breathed in and out, trying to summon the strength to keep talking, to try and convince him to come back. *If you leave now,* I thought, *then you are leaving for good. It's over.*

Sometimes I have to remind myself how hard it is for Anil to be in Taiwan. He's used to neatness and order, being the master of his own schedule, being able to say what he thinks. In Taiwan we're constrained and completely dependent on other people. And while neither of us speaks the language, at least I have the advantage of looking like everyone else, of not being pegged as a foreigner because of the color of my skin. I take for granted the ability to walk around with a certain ease and anonymity while he attracts unwanted attention wherever we go.

At least once a day he'll say to me: "Did you see that man/ woman/child giving me a dirty look?" But somehow I never notice until the offending person has already disappeared from view. I want to empathize with him, but the truth is that I have a hard time seeing him as others see him.

While it's no longer unusual to see white foreigners on the streets of Taipei, there are very few people of color. And although Anil is of Indian descent, because of his shaved head, people often mistake him for African American—even at home in the States. He's aware that he sticks out, that people will always look at him with undisguised curiosity. They don't see him as another kind of Asian or as a dutiful Taiwanese son-in-law.

But I'm oblivious to puzzled or unfriendly stares. I look at him and simply see my husband—handsome and smart, practical and action oriented, occasionally hot tempered but only because he cares.

That evening, after I finally convinced Anil to stay, I went over to the fourth-floor apartment to help my dad prepare for Herlina's arrival. The apartment was a hopeless mess; my dad had been refusing help for months, and since he only received visitors at the ninth-floor apartment, no one knew how bad things were at the fourth floor. It helped that I had a specific goal: to clear out my mom's study to make a bedroom for Herlina. Otherwise I would have felt engulfed by the chaos that penetrated every room, like a river overflowing its banks.

My dad attempted to straighten up the living room and coffee table while my mom watched TV. I waded into the sea of piled-up papers, books, shopping bags, and clothes in my mom's study. There was no time to thoughtfully sort the important stuff (private letters, published articles, photos) from the junk (church programs, used-up notepads, old newspapers) or to find the appropriate place to deposit each item.

I turned myself into a human excavator truck, scooping up raw material from the study and transporting it to the tatami room, which had become a makeshift storage area. Books, magazines, documents, and anything flat or square got piled up in tall stacks. Dirty clothes were thrown into a laundry basket. Anything that wasn't stackable was stuffed into sturdy shopping bags and wedged into a corner of the tatami room. I approached the task with a zen-like concentration, and the repetitive motions of moving and stacking helped me forget about the trauma of my argument with Anil.

Working as fast as I could, it still took me a couple of hours to clear a reasonable space. I grew increasingly sweaty and sticky and began coughing from all the dust I breathed in. My eyes were watering too. But the worst was getting to the bottom of a pile and seeing something scurry away between the bookcases.

"Aaaaaah!" I shrieked.

"What's wrong?" my dad asked.

"I saw a cockroach!"

As each pile disappeared from the floor and more carpet was revealed, I discovered more unpleasant surprises: a huge spider, a dead cockroach, and something I'd never seen before, what

looked like a small shimmering caterpillar—a silverfish. I shud-
dered, too scared to kill it and flush it down the toilet. I worried
about my mom's priceless collection of oversized art books, her
scholarly books on feminism and theology, and my dad's biblical reference books in the next room. What if there was a major
infestation?

"Dad, do you have a vacuum cleaner?"

"Don't worry about that. It's too late now. I'll do it tomorrow
morning."

"Okay. Do you need anything else?"

I was desperate to leave. My clothes were sticking to me, and
my hands were dirty. I also needed to pee, but the bathroom was
so filthy that I didn't want to use it. I forced myself to hold my
bladder until I could get back to the ninth floor.

"Actually, yes. Come in here," he said, pointing me to the
bedroom.

"Can you go through all these drawers and find all of Mom's
jewelry? I want to put it into a box so I can lock it up."

My dad went back out to the living room and sat with my
mom. One by one, I pulled open the drawers of her vanity table
and lifted out handfuls of small boxes and pouches filled with
necklaces, bracelets, and brooches, along with a few pairs of clip-
on earrings. There were expensive pearls and precious stones
mixed in with strands of ethnic beads and cheap costume jewelry. I tried to consolidate similar items in fewer boxes to maximize the space. Everything had to fit in a large metal biscuit tin
that my dad was going to use as a safe.

I thought it was wise that my dad was stashing my mom's
jewelry out of reach of the housekeeper. But I was also sad to be
packing up these remnants of my mom's former self. She had collected these pieces over decades—some handed down from her

own mother, some given to her by my dad, souvenirs from his many trips abroad.

My mom didn't care for displays of status; there were no flashy diamonds or designer watches or ostentatious rings. She was fond of jewelry as adornment, the way she was fond of silk scarves and nice belts. These were items that represented her personality and her taste. But none of them meant anything to her anymore; she no longer wore any jewelry or makeup and would not notice their absence.

Later that night, back on the ninth floor, Anil held me in his arms and begged for my forgiveness. We had been apart for several hours while I helped clean the fourth-floor apartment, and the solitude helped to clear his head.

"I'm sorry, I'm sorry . . ."

I was snuggled up to his chest but facing away from him on the hard, unyielding mattress in the ninth-floor bedroom, still numb from our fight.

"I don't know what happened, I just lost it . . ."

I nodded without saying anything. My face was swollen from crying. My whole body was limp from exhaustion. I acknowledged his apology silently, afraid to admit how scared I still was. It was as though we had been on an airplane that suddenly plunged 10,000 feet, and we were about to say our goodbyes when the airplane righted itself again. Part of me was still in freefall, unable to believe that the danger had passed.

Do you know how close we came to the edge? Do you know how close we came to losing each other?

Another Incident

We left Taiwan in late October, returning to our half-furnished apartment, still filled with dozens of moving boxes stacked three-deep in every room. I went to work the next morning, climbing back onto the corporate treadmill of nonstop meetings and deadlines. Though we had only been gone for ten days, I felt like I was coming back from an epic journey. Things were exactly as I left them, yet nothing was the same.

I kept myself busy. My job was so demanding that I rarely had time to reflect during the day. Every evening and weekend we unpacked more boxes and took inventory of what was still needed for the apartment. We spent countless hours searching online and in stores for the perfect room divider, the ideal desk for my home office, and an attractive rug that was big enough for our living room but still affordable. Furnishing and finishing the apartment became an obsession.

Sometime after we came back, I began having chest pains. They would strike without warning in the middle of a workday. I'd be taking a walk at lunchtime, pondering some work-related issue, when I'd be caught off guard by the thought of my parents' suffering halfway around the world. Usually I was good at compartmentalizing—keeping that distant reality walled off from my day-to-day life. But suddenly there were cracks that allowed my worst fears to come flying to the surface: *What if my mom runs away again? What if my dad can't cope? What if she has to be put in a nursing home?* My chest would tighten, and I would gasp for air, trying to prevent myself from being submerged, swept under a wall of water threatening to overpower me.

The tears would well up, and I wouldn't see the person from my office saying hello until just after she walked by, when I'd return the greeting a second too late. I would try to compose myself before going back into the building, willing the darkness to retreat. Then I'd put on my game face for the elevator ride up thirty-two floors, forcing myself to smile. *Hey, long time no see! How's it going? I'm fine, I'm fine.*

I confided in a few people about how difficult the trip was, but mostly I went on with my life, immersing myself in familiar routines. On the outside, I was able to maintain the illusion that things were okay, but internally I was falling apart. My face erupted in terrible breakouts. I began grinding my teeth in my sleep. I had nightmares about being naked in public, typical anxiety dreams about shame and fear of exposure. I was guarding a dark secret about my family, an ugly truth that I didn't want anyone to know about. But the more I pushed it down, the more it hurt me from the inside, infecting my skin and sucking the breath from my lungs.

I read a book about Alzheimer's by Eleanor Cooney entitled *Death in Slow Motion,* which is a fitting description of the prolonged agony endured by family members. Every day we lost my mom more and more; distance and disorientation grew. Each little failure robbed her of dignity and robbed us of the person we knew. After our visit to Taiwan, these losses were no longer abstract; they were frighteningly real.

And so I did everything I could to avoid confronting the monster in my gut. I ignored it, suppressed it, tried to keep it hidden in the hopes that I could diminish its power. The monster isn't my mom, with her bizarre moods and delusions. It isn't even the cruel disease that's stealing her away from us, little by little.

The monster that I can't bear to face is my grief.

A few days after Thanksgiving, about a month after we returned from Taiwan, Auntie Huichin sent me a lengthy email.

Hi, Ted, Grace, and Anil,
Uncle and I came back from Sanhsia late last night (Nov. 29). I am very sorry to tell you that your parents experienced a very stressful day yesterday. I wonder whether anyone has told you.

Your mother got lost for 6 hours from midnight of Nov. 28 till early morning of Nov. 29. Fortunately patrol policemen found her in Yingge (the pottery town next to Sanhsia) and called an ambulance to bring her to the emergency room of Un-chu-kong Hospital in Sanhsia around 6:00 a.m. We were told that her face was covered with blood. There was also blood on her dress and jacket. Her eyeglasses were broken, support stockings and high heels were torn, and there were bruises and cuts on her face, a big lump on left hip, bruises and blisters on her feet. The doctors put stitches above her left eyebrow and chin. Sorry, I did not ask how many stitches, even though I was there with her in the emergency room.

I suppose you want to know how did it happen. Your mother had become rather restless on Monday afternoon (Nov. 28). Your father went out with her to walk twice, with Lina following behind. The third time he let Lina go out with her. I went out with her one more time after dinner, with Lina following behind. She seemed to be calm after that, so I went up to the ninth floor apartment and had a long telephone conversation with your Aunt Emi.

Shortly before midnight, your mother became restless again and wanted to go out. Lina wanted to follow, but your father thought she had been walking so much in the afternoon already, so he wanted her to get some rest. They went out together by themselves. As usual, your father could not keep up with your mother, and she began to walk fast ahead. He managed to keep her in sight until she reached Un-chu-kong Hospital, when he lost track of her. He finally called your cousin Un-chun for help. Uncle Ko·-tiū^n and your cousin Êng-iāu began their search on motorcycles while Lina and Un-chun searched on foot. I stayed at the entrance to the apartment complex, in case she came back by herself, and also tried to prevent your father from going out to search again after he came back from the hospital area.

We stopped on foot searching by 1:30 a.m. Un-chun and I went to the police station to give a "missing persons" report. Within 5 minutes the news was transmitted to all the police stations on the island. Your father and Lina stayed up all night to wait. By 4:00 a.m. Êng-iāu decided to stop his search and left the search to the police. Two hours later at 6:00 a.m. we received information that she was found and everybody rushed to the hospital . . .

I called my dad as soon as I could but wasn't able to reach him until almost forty-eight hours after it had all happened. Though I asked him numerous questions, he couldn't tell me much more than my aunt had. He was clearly exhausted and overwhelmed but told me I didn't need to come back to Taiwan again. He and my mom and Lina went to stay in a room at Tōa-ko·'s compound while my mom recovered, so they would be close to relatives if they needed any help.

A few days later, when I was at work, I received an email with a batch of photos from my cousin Un-chun. Reluctantly, I clicked on the attached photos, all extreme close-ups of my mom's face when she was in the hospital. Even though I knew she was in bad shape, I could not have anticipated how terrible she looked: she had two black eyes, and her face was swollen and covered with cuts and yellow bruises. Her eyes were closed in each shot; if I didn't know better, I would have thought I was looking at a corpse.

My mom doesn't remember what happened the night she got lost. Was she struck by a car while wandering on the highway? Did she fall and hit her face? Was she assaulted by a stranger or attacked by a stray dog? Not knowing what caused her injuries compounded my anguish, and I couldn't stop imagining violent scenarios. Anything could have happened in those desolate hours between midnight and sunrise. All we know for sure is that she is lucky she survived.

Anil didn't understand why I wanted to see the photos, and he was angry with my cousin for sending me such traumatic images. I explained that I needed to confront the reality of what happened to her.

I closed the email and tried to go back to work, but the images continued to haunt me. I didn't tell anyone at work. I had told my friends about the first time my mom got lost, but this time I kept it mostly to myself. They would ask me how my mom was, and I would say something vague about coping the best we could. The second incident was simply too awful, too unreal for there to be any kind of polite, sympathetic response.

Part of it was that I didn't want to admit—to myself or any-one else—that despite our best efforts, things were getting worse. So I swallowed this knowledge like a razor blade, thinking I would rather bleed invisibly than disturb anyone else with this nightmare.

My chest pains continued, and I began to wonder if some-thing other than stress was responsible. Was I having a heart attack? Was it something I was eating or drinking? Was it due to poor sleep? One night when I was home alone, I researched my symptoms on the internet and thought about whether there was a connection to something I hadn't considered.

The last time I had felt intense pain was the previous Mon-day. It felt like someone was sitting on my chest. I could barely breathe. At the time, I thought it was due to an argument I'd had with Anil the night before. It was a trivial issue that he had blown out of proportion. I had grabbed a blanket to sleep on the futon in my home office while he went to sleep in our bedroom.

Other times when we've had fights and tried to sleep sepa-rately, one of us would always emerge after a while to implore the other person to come back to bed. He always said he couldn't sleep without me next to him, even when we were mad at each other, so we had never actually slept apart until that Sunday night. I was cold and uncomfortable on the futon, and my whole body ached the next day.

I had thought my chest was hurting and I was having trou-ble breathing because I was sad and because I had slept terribly. The following day was when I got the email telling me about my mom's disappearance. It suddenly occurred to me that my pain roughly coincided with the time my mom went missing—late morning/early afternoon in California is the middle of the night in Taiwan. Was I suffocating when she was out wandering the streets, bleeding and bruised? Was my body aching as she suffered alone, lost to her husband, to the world, to herself?

I began to sob. I was gasping for air as the pain came over me again, and then a new insight. She was running away from my dad, who had become—of necessity—a controlling presence in her life. Even as her memory and cognitive abilities declined, I could see that she hated the loss of her independence. I wonder if my mom wasn't just running away but also trying to run *to* something—to an earlier, irrecoverable self.

I, too, had spent the night apart from my husband, tortured with doubt. Was I running away as well?

A Seed Doesn't Choose
Where It Falls

Her mother planted the bathtub-sized flower bed with watermelon-red begonias, bright yellow and magenta snapdragons, and dark-orange marigolds. But the flowers she treasured most of all she kept inside on the windowsill—delicate African violets in a deep, jewel-like color that reminded her of velvet.

What does a child know about growing?

If the child is raised in another country, in another language, surrounded by people who don't look like her, she knows only what she can see.

The family lived at the end of a row of brick apartments that faced another row with a communal grass lawn in between. The girl loved to climb the tree just opposite their front door, didn't care that they called her a tomboy. She was allowed to walk around the neighborhood by herself—to school, to the duck pond, or to Krauszer's to buy candy. She wore a spare key on a shoelace around her neck.

They shopped in discount stores, the kind that sell slightly imperfect socks and towels and overstock of last season's coats and boots. On summer weekends, the family went to the Englishtown flea market, where the parents would browse the used books and furniture for hours. It was hot and dusty, but their reward was getting to eat hotdogs and Italian ice. They'd bring home fresh-squeezed apple cider in a plastic jug and the most special treat of all: a bag of mangoes.

Mangoes are cheap and ubiquitous in Taiwan, but in New Jersey in the 1970s they were a luxury—expensive, rare, and delicious. It was her only sensory connection to the place she was born, a precious taste of home. None of the other neighborhood kids had ever tasted a mango. It was sunshine in her mouth. It was contraband, a secret they kept from other families.

One year, her grandmother came to visit from Taiwan. A-má spoke the language she was in the process of forgetting, but they got along easily and watched TV and ate snacks together. A-má knit her a cardigan from yarn the color of ripe tomatoes. The buttons were the size of quarters, and the pockets had laces tied into a bow with pompons dangling from the ends.

She left after a few months, but A-má was proof that Taiwan existed, that you could love something that loved you back, even when you could not see it.

The year before they moved away, what she remembered most was the music: the Bee Gees, Eagles, Foreigner, and Queen played on her brother's portable record player.

Her brother was five years older, so they didn't have much in common, but one thing they did do together was they each planted a mango seed. The seeds were large and flat, bigger than her hand, the shape of a bar of soap when it's more than half used up. They put the seeds in big flowerpots on the front porch and took turns watering them for a year. The saplings were surprisingly sturdy with dark, smooth leaves. Her brother's grew to be about three feet tall while hers languished, several inches shorter, even though they were planted at the same time.

"It's not fair," she said.

When it was time to go, she abandoned the bike she'd only

recently started to ride with training wheels, along with the fledgling mango trees.

In Hong Kong, their apartment was a little bigger, but instead of a grassy yard and trees, they shared a cramped stairwell and elevator with dozens of families. They lived on the sixth floor of a high-rise building. Hundreds of people shared the same address; everything was vertical.

Instead of a porch and flower bed, there was a tiled balcony with a view of the harbor and Kai Tak International Airport. Her mother cultivated a different set of plants here, more suited to the humid tropical climate. The girl did not know the names of any of them, but she has photos of her mom standing on the balcony at night holding two spiky white flowers.

"They only bloom at night, once a year!" her mom told the girl.

The girl lived there for ten years—a long time. But who's counting? At that age, her attention was focused in only one direction: forward. She was waiting for her life to begin.

She wore the red cardigan from A-má until she couldn't button it anymore and her wrists poked out. One summer they went back to New Jersey for a visit. They drove by their old neighborhood, parked the car, and got out to look around. The tree she used to climb was still there. It was much taller now, but when she went to climb it, she found that the branches had multiplied and thickened, and she could no longer maneuver easily in between them.

It is the first loss she remembers.

The girl became a young woman, moved to California, went to

college, got a boyfriend, got a job. Another boyfriend. Another job. They accumulated.

This was how she measured time in her twenties, by the length of her entanglements. Her aperture widened, taking in more of the world, and she defined herself by how much distance she could cover, roaming to places her parents had never been—the Côte d'Azur, the Great Barrier Reef. This felt like knowledge.

She visited her parents in Taiwan almost every year and once spent a whole summer with them at their house on Yangmingshan. The house was old and quirky, but her mom had more room for the plants she liked to cultivate. Now that the children were grown up and had moved out, her mom had more time for the things she enjoyed.

Her mom's favorite plant was a kind of cactus whose flower bloomed only once a year, in the dark. Her mom lovingly tended to the plant, and each evening at dinnertime she gave updates, saying with growing anticipation, "It's almost ready." Several nights in a row her mom stayed up late, reading a book or grading her seminary students' papers while checking her flowers to detect the slightest shift in their tightly wound buds, careful not to let any mosquitos in when she opened the front door. Then one night she noticed the buds had picked up their heads almost imperceptibly, turning away from each other to allow space for the white petals to slowly unfurl.

"Jin! Jin!" Her mom called her dad to get the camera and pleaded with him to stay up an extra hour to wait for the flowers to reach their full glory under the moonlight.

A day later, after the flowers had wilted, they were added to a brothy soup. She remembered it tasted like a silky, perfumy onion.

The daughter never learned the name of the flower. There were a lot of things in Taiwan that she could not name, like her favorite sautéed vegetable, or the sweet, amber-colored drink they were sometimes served in restaurants. She didn't even know the proper names of any of her relatives; she knew them only by their birth order, their position and status in the family tree.

Even though her parents had lived abroad for more than twenty years, when they returned to Taiwan they simply resumed their place in the family hierarchy, a structure that to her seemed as stable and immovable as a mountain. She, on the other hand, stayed in California but doubted her commitment. The longest she stayed with a boyfriend was seven years. The longest she held a job was four. It never occurred to her to keep plants or pets because she didn't know how long she would stay.

Looking back, it seemed foolish that her mom had let her plant a mango tree all those years ago, when they lived in the wrong climate and knew they would never see the fruit. Why even start when they were bound to be disappointed?

At twenty weeks, a fetus is the size of a banana.

This was how long she waited until telling her parents that she was pregnant. (The year before she'd made the mistake of telling them too soon, and then she'd lost the pregnancy. She did not want to take that chance again.)

She flew to Taiwan and told them in person, just when her baby bump was beginning to show, after she'd been through all the testing and passed all the milestones, when she could finally exhale and allow herself to be happy, to anticipate the life growing inside her.

For nine months, she counted everything in weeks. After the baby was born, she counted everything in months. Each small increment mattered, was a point scored toward viability, strength, survival.

She celebrated her forty-first birthday with her parents in Taiwan. The baby was two years old, bright-eyed, and easy to amuse with toys, songs, and cake. The aunties and cousins passed him around, and for the first time in months she enjoyed the luxury of having her hands free.

They had just finished eating cake when her brother called and told her the news: he had been diagnosed with liver cancer and would not be able to join them in Taiwan.

The tumor was the size of a mango. Nine months later, he was gone.

Three years after her mom passed away, she learned the name of the flower, though it goes by many names: queen of the night, night-blooming cereus, tan hua, epiphyllum. One summer day she took her son, now nine years old, to the San Francisco Epiphyllum Society's Annual Flower Show in Golden Gate Park. They browsed the tables and sighed over the prizewinning blooms displayed in mason jars filled with water. So many colors: creamy white, pale pink, hot pink, yellow, and even purple.

"This was Grandma's favorite flower," she told him.

They bought some cuttings, which would take two or three years to flower, and a small bag of soil. She decided it was worth a try. They put the paddle-shaped cuttings into small plastic pots on their deck and watered them weekly, a shared labor of love.

Occasionally she forgot. Or they went on vacation and didn't instruct the house sitter to water them because they worried about the cat escaping or the house sitter getting locked out. The leaves grew bigger and sprouted new leaves, but the time between watering grew longer and longer, until she stopped completely. Doubt took over.

She apologized to her son. She knew she would fail.

The summer of the pandemic is the first summer the family has not traveled at all, has not even left their zip code except for one time when they drove through a desolate, empty San Francisco. Their experience of the world consists of taking long walks through the hills where they live. They satisfy their desire for stimulation by observing small seasonal changes around them— a neighbor renovating their house, wild blackberries ripening on the vine, fawns losing their spots as they get braver and bigger, camelia trees in full flower and then decay.

Stuck at home with nowhere to go, it seems as though all activity has ground to a halt—until they go outside and see that nature never takes a vacation, it is always throbbing and multiplying unseen, regardless of our wishes.

How foolish to think that growth only happens when we decide we are ready for it.

After six months in isolation, her son's hair is shaggy, and his pants are too short. She offers to cut his hair, but he says *no,* offers to buy him new clothes, but he says, *what's the point?* Her husband keeps referring to it as "the lost year." It feels as though time is standing still, and yet, the boy's feet are now the same size as hers, and she is certain that he will be as tall as her by his next birthday.

One summer morning, she woke up as usual and went upstairs to feed the cat. She hadn't yet brushed her teeth and was not wearing her glasses. Out of the corner of her eye she caught a flash of pink on the corner of her deck, the deck she hadn't even bothered to sit on all summer long.

The epiphyllum she had abandoned—hadn't thought about in months—had bloomed unexpectedly, roaring to life in a blazing shade of hot pink, demanding an audience for her brief but hard-won glory.

Allegories

1. The Little Mermaid

I am eight years old. We are Taiwanese immigrants in New Jersey—my father, mother, older brother, and me. It's the late 1970s, and I am watching a TV adaptation of Hans Christian Andersen's "The Little Mermaid"—not the Disney version, but one created by Toei, a Japanese animation studio.

I'm enchanted by this tale of a young mermaid who falls in love with a human prince whose life she saved after his ship is wrecked in a violent storm. She dreams of becoming human so that she can marry him, so she goes to the Sea Witch and trades her voice for a magic potion that will cause her fishtail to separate into legs—a painful transformation. She leaves her mother and sisters behind, drinks the potion and is reunited with the prince, but his interest in her is only platonic.

I identify with the mermaid's mute perseverance, her ability to blend in and hide her origins, her otherness. I, too, left my home and forgot the songs of my ancestors, the language I was born with. My parents still communicate in Taiwanese, but I can no longer call it forth. Like the mermaid's tail, it remains hidden deep inside me like a vestigial organ, like a blueprint that will never be used.

Growing up, I have a lifelong need to be close to the ocean. But I am the one who is shipwrecked.

2. Psyche

I am twelve years old. We have lived in Hong Kong for two years, and though I look like the people around me, I remain a foreigner who attends an American school and speaks only English. At the school's annual book fair, I pick up a paperback with a blue cover called *Till We Have Faces* by C. S. Lewis, a fictional first-person retelling of the Cupid and Psyche myth told from the point of view of Psyche's protective older sister, Orual.

Psyche, the youngest daughter of the King of Glome, grows up to be the most beautiful maiden in the kingdom, rivaling the goddess Aphrodite, who becomes jealous. Aphrodite sends her naughty son Cupid to wound Psyche with one of his love arrows and make her fall in love with a beast, but instead of piercing her, he accidentally wounds himself and falls in love with her. He secretly whisks Psyche away to a beautiful castle where she is lavished with attention by an invisible host—Cupid himself, who makes her promise never to seek his identity.

When Orual pays a visit to the castle, she persuades Psyche that any husband who refuses to show himself must be a hideous monster. Psyche agrees to light an oil lamp when her husband comes for his nightly visit in order to see his true face, but this has disastrous consequences and leads to a harrowing journey where she must complete a series of impossible tasks, including sorting a giant mountain of mixed grain and fetching a box of beauty from the underworld to give to Aphrodite.

I empathize with Psyche, who is taken from her family and thrust into a bewildering new life, only to have that revoked as well. I, too, have experienced a double loss: New Jersey was nothing like Taiwan. Hong Kong was nothing like New Jersey. Like Psyche in the wilderness, I have no guide to help me navigate. Being a third-culture kid means being misunderstood and out of place, a seed planted in the wrong soil, swept up in a story that I didn't choose. I spend years looking for an idea of "home" in somebody else, not realizing I need to seek it within myself first. Although I lack a template, I eventually build a life for myself, grain by grain.

3. Persephone

I am in my twenties, living in San Francisco after graduating from university. My parents have moved from Hong Kong back to Taiwan; I visit them almost every year. Taking the red-eye from SFO to TPE is disorienting no matter how many times I do it. While I'm dreaming, we cross the International Date Line, where one day skips ahead to the next. My brain understands the time change, but my body does not, and I feel upside down for days. Arriving in Taiwan, I have the bizarre sensation of going forward in linear time yet backward in consciousness, reaching for a distant, earlier version of myself that once felt at home here.

I've met my Taiwanese relatives countless times over the years. I move among these people who share a name and resemblance with me, but because of the language barrier I'm always an outsider. They serve me gorgeous platters of fruit—guava, pineapple, papaya, mango—and I eat while hardly saying a word. When I meet and marry my husband, my visits to Taiwan diminish.

This constant cycle of travel and return reminds me of the myth of Demeter and Persephone. Like Persephone, I am the eternal daughter, destined to go back and forth between my husband in California and my parents in Taiwan, between the life consciously chosen and the collective unconscious that claims me, an unbreakable thread connecting me to my ancestors. I live in a constant state of longing to be reunited with Demeter—my mother, motherland, mother tongue. My life is defined by this rupture.

4. Inanna

I am in my thirties, working as a freelance writer and editor in Oakland, when my mom begins having cognitive issues. At first she laughs it off and makes jokes about getting old and senile, and we go along with it. But there are cracks in her brave façade; at times she looks worried, too, aware that things are slipping but unable to explain why.

As her lapses become more frequent and my dad worries he can no longer leave her alone, her world becomes gradually smaller and more circumscribed, and my dad's along with it. Before long, her orbit is restricted to four places: home, my aunt's house, the doctor's office, and church. She stops cooking and cleaning. Her hygiene suffers. But it's not until my mom runs away one night and gets lost and injured on a remote mountain path that any of us see the gravity of her condition, the frightening reality of what it's like to be losing your memory and identity with each passing day.

One summer, I sign up for a course on Jungian psychology called Separation, Sorrow and Individuation, and I am introduced to the myth of Inanna, the ancient Sumerian Queen of Heaven, a goddess of extraordinary power and radiance thought to be an antecedent to the Greek Aphrodite. The most well-known story of Inanna, referenced in the *Epic of Gilgamesh* and in the poems of Enheduanna, is her descent to the underworld to visit her sister Ereshkigal. Inanna puts on her full regalia, including a turban, lapis lazuli necklace, beaded breastplate, girdle, and golden ring to signify her divine status. On her way down to the underworld she must pass through seven gates, surrendering one of her royal garments each time until she is rendered ordinary, robbed of her beauty, brought low before being allowed to meet her sister, the Queen of the Underworld.

I burst into tears in the middle of the psychology class because I suddenly recognize my mother and the violent stripping away of all her worldly knowledge, her skills and manners, her status and achievements—her very identity. Inanna dies a symbolic death in the underworld, but she is revived by her faithful companion, Ninshubur, who sprinkles the food and water of life on her corpse to break the spell and bring her back to the upper world.

I, however, cannot reverse the decline. I have no magic that will physically bring my mom back to wholeness, back to life. My only choice is to re-member her, to re-constitute her, through my writing.

Last Time in Bangkok

The immediate family members were invited into the small, windowless room, covered floor-to-ceiling in bright blue tiles. The only decoration was a high, small alcove displaying a crucifix and a simple bouquet. This was not how I expected to see my brother, lying on a platform, wearing a dark blue suit, covered up to his chest in a white sheet. His arms were straight by his side and his hands looked dark and unnaturally big. Makeup disguised his yellowed skin, and he was clean-shaven. He was still wearing his glasses, and his eyes were shut in peaceful repose. His face had been gaunt in the photos my uncle took in the hospital the previous week, and my husband had commented on how handsome Ted looked with more chiseled features. But today his cheeks were plumped up again, and I wondered if that was the embalmer's craft, trying to make the deceased look as much as possible like his portrait, like the stocky, muscular man everyone remembered.

In January 2010, I went with my husband and son to visit my parents in Taiwan. I had advised them not to make a big deal out of my birthday, but my cousin's wife found out about it and invited us over for an informal dinner in my honor. I am smiling in the photos, posing with chopsticks in midair, holding "long life" noodles. We took a few family portraits as well—Anil and I standing behind my mom and dad, the four of us looking at the camera while two-year-old Devin leans forward in his highchair to get closer to the strawberries-and-cream birthday cake.

We were eating cake when my brother called. Ted had lived in Bangkok for almost two decades; his wife was Thai, and his children were bilingual. He was scheduled to arrive in Taipei the next day. He didn't visit my parents often, but when he did, he tried to plan his trips to coincide with mine. I heard my dad say, "What? What?" into his cell phone, and then, "you better talk to Grace." He handed the phone to me. My brother explained that he was not coming to Taiwan after all, that he had been feeling unwell and visited the doctor a few days earlier—something he rarely did. Several tests and x-rays later, he was diagnosed with a tumor the size of a large mango. It was in his liver and had been completely undetected until it began to press against his kidneys.

I walked into the next room so I could hear better, but even then the words didn't sink in. Ted calmly explained what the doctors had told him about this type of cancer and his treatment options. "The liver is the only organ that can regenerate itself," he said with the conviction of a lifelong gambler, someone who always thought he could beat the odds. "The prognosis is mixed, but I'm not worried. I could have years left." The doctors thought surgery might work, but only if my brother made immediate lifestyle changes: he needed to quit smoking and take medication to manage his hepatitis and undiagnosed diabetes. They would evaluate him again in two months.

"Do the kids know?" I asked. My brother had two daughters aged sixteen and fourteen, and a nine-year-old son.

He paused. "Not really . . . They know something is wrong, but they don't know what."

For nine months, Ted underwent chemotherapy and various other treatments. I kept in touch with him via Skype and email and was surprised to hear that he was well enough to keep working and traveling through the summer (he commuted between his home in Bangkok and his office in Singapore, where he worked for an international gaming consultancy).

I emailed my brother articles about recently passed US healthcare reform and the high-risk pool, just in case he was eligible to return to the States for treatment. I inquired about the political unrest in Bangkok. I asked the dreaded but necessary questions: Do you have life insurance? (No.) Do the kids have legal status in Thailand? (No.) Will your wife get a job? (No.) At one point, he learned that his company was behind on payroll, had negative cash flow, and was going to lay off all its employees. While my anxiety mounted, Ted remained stubbornly optimistic. He saw it as just another setback rather than a crisis.

The doctors reversed their initial recommendation and did not perform surgery since the cancer had spread, so their focus turned to killing the cancer cells. Ted applied for a patient assistance program to get subsidized access to Nexavar, which would otherwise cost six thousand dollars per month. In August, my dad wired him twenty thousand dollars to pay for an experimental procedure called selective internal radiation therapy, in which high doses of radioactive microspheres are injected directly into the tumor.

The SIR-spheres procedure went well, but in September, Ted was hospitalized again. When he didn't improve after more than a week and was too weak to carry on a phone conversation, I knew I had to go to Bangkok. I booked the ticket on Friday and departed San Francisco on Tuesday. I persuaded my dad—over his protests that it would be too difficult to travel due to his advanced Parkinson's—to meet me in Bangkok. "It may be our last chance," I told him.

I spent the fourteen-hour flight reading magazines and watching movies, unable to sleep, unwilling to focus on the task in front of me. What does one say to a dying brother? We had never been especially close, and we spoke rarely, although the frequency increased after I found out he was sick. I had visited him in Bangkok a few times over the years, and he had come to San Francisco for my wedding and after Devin was born. Except for those few trips, we were barely involved in each other's lives. We had not lived on the same continent for more than twenty years. But something far stronger than reason tugged at me to go to his side.

I arrived in Bangkok after midnight on Wednesday. When I emerged from immigration and baggage claim, no one was there to greet me. I started walking through the terminal to see if my brother's family was waiting at another meeting spot. From a distance, I saw Ted's eldest daughter, Jenny, her brother, Billy, and their mom. I greeted Jenny first with a hug.

"Did you hear the news about Dad?" she asked.

"No. What?"

"He passed away last night," she said matter-of-factly.

I put my hand over my mouth and started to cry. She said she sent an email the day before, but it must have been after I'd gotten on the plane. I was too late.

"I'm so sorry," I said, choking up. "Don't worry, I will help you."

In the taxi, Jenny asked polite questions about my flight and my family, as though this were an ordinary conversation. I was amazed at her composure. She explained that she was "all cried out" from the day before. The funeral was set for the next day,

Thursday. My dad was already in Bangkok, and my Uncle I-to had flown in earlier that day. While I was inflight, oblivious to the news that awaited me, everything had already been arranged.

We got to their apartment after one o'clock in the morning. It was too late to call Anil, and I hadn't succeeded in reaching him while on layover in Hong Kong. It occurred to me that he already knew—that my entire family had read Jenny's email by now—and that I was the last to find out.

Almost everyone was asleep already, but my dad came out to greet me. I hugged him and apologized for not getting there sooner. There wasn't much else to say. He looked so weak and diminished—back bent, chest hollow, hair unkempt. He could barely lift his head enough to look me in the eye. It had been a very long day.

Everyone was unusually restrained. They'd had twenty-four hours to process the news, but I was still in shock. Eight of us were crowded into the apartment: my sister-in-law and the three kids in one bedroom, my dad and uncle in the second bedroom, and me and my cousin Un-chun (who chaperoned my dad) in the third. Though the apartment was large by Thai standards, there wasn't enough space to hold all the emotion. It was all too much, and yet it was so quiet since it was the middle of the night.

After taking a shower, I went into the bedroom as quietly as possible and crawled into bed, wide awake. I was staying in what had been Ted's bedroom, next to Un-chun, who was already asleep. A long cylindrical pillow served as a divider in the middle of the mattress. I tried not to dwell on the fact that I was sleeping in a dead man's bed.

At two o'clock in the morning, Jenny was still awake, sitting on the sofa looking through old family albums: photo after photo of two smiling girls with pigtails, their proud mom, their baby brother. Ted was mostly absent from these pages since he was usually the one behind the camera. The last thing I remember was hearing Jenny's cell phone or computer chirp from time to time with a new instant message.

I woke up before six o'clock but didn't get out of bed until I heard voices. Un-chun was still asleep. I went out and said good morning to my niece Shelly, my dad, and Uncle I-to. My dad stood up slowly and paused before taking a step, in case he got dizzy. He had his insulin shot first, then a handful of pills. We ate breakfast in silence—fried eggs with a splash of Knorr sauce, toast, and sweetened instant coffee. I convinced my dad to let me change his flight from Friday to Saturday so that we'd have more time together. I called the airline, but the reservations desk wasn't open yet.

When I packed for my trip, I chose casual, light-colored clothes. Thailand was hot and humid, and I made a conscious decision to avoid my usual dark, urban uniform. I briefly considered bringing a black dress but ultimately decided against it. The irony hit me that morning when I realized I had nothing appropriate to wear to the funeral.

Ted's wife kindly offered to lend me something to wear. She, too, was incredibly composed, focused intently on taking care of her kids and in-laws to suppress a tidal wave of grief. Ted's death left her not only without a husband, but without any means of support. She brought over a handful of hangers with black dresses and blouses—I was surprised that she didn't have more black clothing. Then again, she may have only chosen things that would fit me, since she was much more petite than I. She and the girls wore simple black dresses. In the handful of outfits she gave me, there was one black and white sleeveless lace dress that I liked, but it seemed too pretty, too cheerful to wear to such an occasion. Instead I chose a plain black blouse with a ruffled placket and pearl buttons to wear with my black pants. The buttons strained across my chest, so I had to keep my breathing shallow.

After I was dressed and ready, I cracked open Jenny's laptop to quickly check my email. Even though I really wanted to talk to Anil and Devin, there wasn't enough time for Skype. We were in a rush to get to the hospital by eight thirty, and there was no privacy anyway, no space in which to confront my emotions.

My dad was the last to be ready. Jenny said, "Grandpa can't stop crying." I went into the bedroom and saw my usually stoic dad sitting on the edge of the bed, head bent over, eyes closed. I don't remember ever seeing him cry, not even at his own mother's funeral. I ran my hand over his back and gave him a long hug, not knowing what to say. I'm sure his grief was compounded by the fact that my mom—by now in the advanced stages of Alzheimer's and needing care around the clock—was not there to support him. He could not even share with her his deep sorrow over the death of their son; she would neither comprehend nor remember. He was mourning for two.

When we arrived at the hospital, we were greeted by about twenty well-dressed women in black in the waiting room, mostly friends of Ted's wife. Jenny and Shelly were carrying bouquets and trying not to cry. Billy stuck by his mother's side.

We went downstairs to the room where they kept Ted's body draped in a white sheet, a sort of makeshift chapel.

We all stood around on one side of the receiving area and listened to a short prayer service in Thai presided over by Rev. Srisuwan, a friend of Uncle I-to. My dad sat in a wheelchair provided by the hospital for the service. Un-chun videotaped the whole thing as though it were another piano recital or birthday dinner. I couldn't bring myself to take out my camera.

I stood there silently crying, while Ted's wife wailed over her husband and the kids cried, "Daddy! Daddy!" I went up closer and touched my brother's shoulder, and said, "I'm sorry I didn't get here in time." I wanted to say more, but there were too many people around, and I didn't want to break the flow of the ceremony.

We left the room again and waited while they lowered my brother's body into a white casket. Four men went into the room, and each took a corner of the bed sheet he was lying on, hoisted it up, then lowered him carefully into an improbably small and flimsy-looking white box. Ted's wife and the kids wailed. The men put the cover into place and then began to seal the box with white tape. I leaned over and asked my dad, "Why are they sealing the box? I thought there was going to be another viewing at the church."

Rev. Srisuwan explained that it was just a precaution to prevent the body from moving while in transit from the hospital to the church where the funeral service would be performed. The men carried the casket and loaded it into a waiting van. The family got into two separate cars for the ride to the church. "Just relax," someone told me. "With traffic it will probably take one hour or more to get there. You can sleep."

I sat in the third row of the car with the minister's wife. She spoke in Taiwanese to my dad, Un-chun, and her husband in the front seat, but we did not speak to each other. I looked out the window as we passed shopping malls, outdoor restaurants, and car dealerships on the way to the toll freeway. Giant billboards advertised TV shows, new high-rise condos, soft drinks, iPhones. Every so often among the maze of small streets and nondescript apartment blocks, a large portrait of King Bhumipol or Queen Sirikit would adorn a municipal hospital, school, or sports stadium, and the glittering ornamentation and swooping lines of a Thai Buddhist temple would break up the grid-like monotony.

From the freeway, an endless series of signs announced, "Welcome to Suvarnabhumi Airport," yet I never actually saw the airport or any airplanes. It seemed we were constantly approaching while never arriving there; everything in Bangkok seemed to be measured in terms of distance from this mythical destination.

Gradually the buildings began to thin out as we reached the outskirts of the city. Vendors sold fruit from roadside stands, and we drove past a couple of cemeteries and stores selling altars and funerary sculptures. The road narrowed to one lane, bordered by the freeway on the right and what looked like rice paddies to the left. Then finally we saw a sign for the church, and we made a left turn up a dirt road.

By then it was almost eleven o'clock and the sun was beating down. We climbed out of the cool, shaded, air-conditioned car into the white heat of the parking lot. Although we were only a few steps away from the church entrance, we opened a parasol for my dad and fanned ourselves furiously in the hundred-degree heat as we walked up to the church.

Outside the entrance, we took off our shoes and walked barefoot onto the clean linoleum. The first thing I noticed were the posterboard signs on the back wall behind the pulpit: "Mr. Ted Loh, Sept. 23, 2010" in English and Thai. Some flower displays and a portrait of my brother were placed on the righthand side below the platform, along with two wooden sawhorses to hold the coffin. An organ stood to the left. Instead of pews there were rows of lightweight stacking chairs. About twenty or thirty people were already there, talking quietly amongst themselves, and more continued to arrive. Several got up to greet Ted's wife and the kids as we entered. My uncle handed us a copy of the program, which was in Thai, as well as a copy of the hymn he planned to sing, which was in Chinese and English.

Four men entered carrying the coffin and set it down on the sawhorses, then they covered it carefully with a white lace sheet.

A part of me still couldn't believe that was my brother in the box, and that he would from this day forward be represented by that framed portrait, reduced to a one-dimensional nine-by-twelve. I was used to seeing my deceased elder relatives in this way, flat images suspended in time and space. But this was someone I lived with for fifteen years, whose voice I clearly remembered out-arguing me or declaring victory over a game of Scrabble. I used to complain bitterly about our clothes being washed in the same load of laundry because the scent of his sweat-soaked athletic uniforms would overpower everything. His famous appetite always dwarfed mine, and his muscular bulk always crossed the imaginary dividing line into my half of the backseat. He was loud, cocky, and opinionated, an outsized presence even to those who only knew him online. My brother was the opposite of a quiet spirit or ghostly ancestor, someone whose flesh-and-bloodness was impossible to deny.

Rev. Srisuwan began the service and welcomed the mourners, then another reverend gave a short sermon, which was partially translated into English by Elder Lee. But the majority of the service was in Thai, and I wondered what it was like for my dad—the multilingual one—to experience what I had been through countless times before, being an outsider due to language. My brother and I were used to being outsiders in Taiwan since we didn't speak Taiwanese. Here in Bangkok, my brother was the one who was assimilated, and my dad and relatives and I were the outsiders who needed help.

Jenny was called up to the stage to say a few words. She got up and addressed the audience, and even though I didn't understand what she was saying, her composure and warmth came through. I recalled for a moment my own wedding, when we had just heard a round of toasts, and people were nudging me, the bride, to say something. But I was too shy, and I regret letting the moment pass without formally expressing my happiness and gratitude to all the people assembled that day. Yet here was Jenny, only sixteen years old, showing such courage and maturity to say a few words at her father's funeral.

Uncle I-to got up onstage to sing the hymn, his contribution to the service. He had composed the music, and the words were written by an American poet. "In the bulb there is a flower, in the seed an apple tree . . ." My cousin Un-chun accompanied him on the organ. Since he sang in English, it was one of the few parts of the service that I completely understood.

The serviced culminated with the casket being opened for a final viewing and mourners being invited to take a rose from a tray and put it into the coffin. Ted's wife went first, followed by Jenny, Shelly, and Billy; and the restraint of the preceding hour was broken by a chorus of "Daddy! Daddy!" This was the final goodbye. After depositing the roses by their father's cheek, the girls stood in front of the casket holding the trays of flowers for the rest of the mourners, their thin bodies trembling with each sob, using their free hands to wipe their tears.

I helped steady my dad as we walked up to the front and placed our flowers into the coffin. I mouthed, "I love you," and paused for a moment to take in the stillness of my brother's face. My dad said, "Go in peace." We sat down again and watched as the rest of the people took their turns, the pile of white roses diminishing one by one as each was placed into the coffin before it was sealed up one last time, unleashing a fresh burst of wailing.

When the service ended, the coffin was carried out a sliding glass door on the right, then loaded through another set of dark glass doors, and then it was lowered down. Only then did I realize that the crematorium was attached to the church, and that those glass doors represented the final exit for my brother's body. I did not go up closer to look. We went over to huddle with the family.

"Do you know what your dad's name means?" my dad asked his grandchildren. They shook their heads.

"'Theodore' means 'God's gift,'" he explained. "Now we are giving him back to God."

The next day, we went to Pattaya to scatter Ted's ashes in a place that he loved. It's a popular beach resort about two hours away from Bangkok. Ted met his wife there, and their family often went there on weekends for fun. I had been there once on a tour in 2001. We drove around for a long time, and I looked at all the signs in the beachside town—real estate, bars, massage parlors, and restaurants catering to every possible nationality. Pattaya had all the hallmarks of an adult playground—lots of bars, scantily clad women, karaoke and cabarets, hotels with suggestive names. All around us was a general whiff of vice.

We drove around from one side of the bay to the other, looking for parking. At one point Ted's wife got out to negotiate the cost of renting a boat. We finally got out of the car and jaywalked across the street to the beach.

The boat was about ten meters off the beach, and we had to take off our shoes and roll our pants up to wade into the shallow water to get on board. Two of us walked on either side of my dad, steadying him. We stopped to consider the best way for him to get on the boat. He considered sitting in a deck chair on the beach and waiting for us to save us the trouble of getting him on and off the boat, but I convinced him it was important for him to come with us. The minister offered to carry my dad piggyback to the boat. I was surprised when my dad accepted the offer, knowing he hates to ask for help or to trouble anyone with his needs. But I was glad that he came with us, and so was he.

We took the boat out a few miles from the beach past the parasailers, and then we stopped about half a mile away from a small island. Jenny and Shelly untied the white bundles—what looked like oversize cloth napkins from a restaurant, each tied up with a ribbon. One bore my brother's leftover bone fragments from the cremation, and the other was filled with ashes. Ted's wife brought along a large traditional silver bowl filled with marigold and white flower petals.

There were ten of us total—Ted's wife, Jenny, Shelly, Billy, me, my dad, Uncle I-to, Un-chun, the minister, and the driver of the boat. All of the family members took turns gathering a handful of Ted's ashes with a handful of the flower petals, and tossing them into the ocean. There was no prayer or ceremony, nor an excess of emotion. The boat motor was idled, and all we could hear was the occasional whir of a camera.

I don't know how many times I dipped my hands into my brother's ashes and cradled the bone fragments. If I thought too hard about it I would recoil, but something told me it was important to get my hands dirty, to fully partake of this silent ritual. It was easier for me—for all of us—to just do it than to reflect on what we were doing, otherwise the emotions would come up.

"Bye, Daddy!" said Billy in a tone that sounded like he was bidding farewell at the airport, to someone who was coming back.

All that was left of my brother's physical being was released into the ocean, blown away by the wind, the flower petals floating on the water being the only visible trace of this final act. Ted's wife and Jenny shook out the white cloths to dispose of everything. I don't know if they reserved any of the ashes to keep with them at home. There was no sink to wash our hands on the boat, so we passed around hand sanitizer and wipes. Once we were done—no more than a half hour after we had arrived—we turned the boat around and motored back to the beach.

We took a few more photos. Again, there was very little conversation, but I took turns hugging Ted's wife, the girls, and Billy. Although it was cloudy and we were returning from a somber task, there was something oddly uplifting about the ride back— the ocean breeze, our hair whipping in the wind, the sound of the motor, the spray hitting our faces. I felt peaceful. We steered past dozens of rainbow-colored parachutes used by the parasailers, floating blithely in the air like airborne jellyfish. I thought as I looked at the family, *Ted wants you to be happy.* And I felt strangely happy and relieved.

Once back on shore, we got back into two cars and drove around for some time looking for a place to have lunch. It was already afternoon, and we were all hungry. We drove from one side of Pattaya to the other side and finally ended up at Pupen Seafood, an open-air restaurant in Jomtien Beach. We ordered a large array of dishes—stir fried crab and shrimp in yellow curry, spicy calamari, sweet and sour fish, shrimp with pea shoots, sautéed vegetables, and two kinds of soup. Although the restaurant wasn't very comfortable—we sat on long, hard benches at heavy wooden tables—the food was outstanding. Even my dad said it was the best meal of the entire trip. It occurred to me later that Ted would have disapproved—he hated seafood. But we ate with gusto until we were full, which in the end was a fitting way to honor him.

Unbridgeable

This is what I hear: The sound of birds screeching. Wind whistling through the trees. The hum of a distant leaf blower. A squirrel landing on a tree branch. The crunch of gravel as someone backs into a driveway. Cars whooshing by on the main road below. What I don't hear is the sound I am waiting for, the sound of a van twisting up my crooked street to pick me up and take me to the airport. I am already late.

It's a quarter to four on Monday afternoon. The airport shuttle was supposed to pick me up between 3:15 and 3:30 p.m., but it came at three o'clock when I was still packing. The driver said he would wait but then left without warning by the time I came upstairs at 3:25 p.m. with my suitcase. I called customer service to complain and ask the van to come back, but they kept putting me on hold and twice disconnected me, and I had to call back yet again and go through all the prompts before being connected to a live human being, who was unsympathetic and told me the van is long gone and no one else is available to come get me.

It's not my fault that I wasn't ready when the van showed up early. I only arranged the trip the night before, after receiving a lengthy email from Uncle I-to saying my dad was admitted to the hospital with an unspecified infection, and my relatives needed me to make a decision about whether or not to authorize feeding tubes, respirators, or other lifesaving measures. I didn't know what to do except to book the next flight to Taiwan. I couldn't pack until the last minute because I spent all morning at Citibank emptying out my dad's account and wiring the money to four accounts at three banks on two continents, just in case, while keeping a poker face and being glad the bank manager did not ask why.

I call for a taxi and the dispatcher says it will be there in ten minutes. After twenty minutes, I call to ask why the taxi has not arrived and the same dispatcher repeats it will be there in ten minutes. So I have no choice but to wait with my suitcase in front of my house on my quiet street in the waning afternoon light and listen to the ambient sounds of my neighborhood, the calm, unhurried rhythms of a day like any other, a perfectly fine day to lose everything I have ever known.

On the plane, I try not to think about what might happen. I spend most of the flight reading *The Year of Magical Thinking* by Joan Didion, which is both an analysis of and a personal reflection on the experience of loss. This is not the kind of book you can read in bits and pieces, in between work and commuting and laundry and birthday parties. It requires what in daily life is impossible: the suspension of time and activity, entering a sort of trance in order to reach the far shore where your head is clear and the meaning of things can sink in.

It is almost midnight when my flight lands at Taipei Taoyuan International Airport, which was renamed in 2006. I have barely slept. Normally, my dad would have met me at the airport or sent a driver or family friend to pick me up and take me to my parents' apartment in Sanhsia. But no one is there to meet me or help me.

I am on my own. It was decided that I would stay with my cousin Un-ho in Taipei. She doesn't speak English, but she has a spare mattress for me to sleep on, and she lives close to the hospital.

I have no idea how to explain to the taxi driver where I am going. I have never been to my cousin's apartment before. All I have is her address in Chinese on my iPhone and a handful of New Taiwan dollars. My uncle said not to pay more than NT$1000 for the ride. The driver squints at my phone in the dark and types the address into his GPS. I'm relieved that I don't have to say anything; technology has spared me the awkward stumbling in a language I barely know.

I'm awake as the taxi navigates the streets of Taipei. The driver turns off the main road into a lane, from the lane into a narrow alley, where he pulls over and waits for me to pay. Now it's my turn to squint at my phone, at the address I cannot read except for the numbers. It is pitch dark and the alley is completely deserted. I drag my suitcase to the end of the alley and somehow I figure out the correct building and apartment number. I punch in my cousin's number on the intercom and am relieved when I hear her voice calling my name.

The next morning, Un-ho takes me to Mackay Memorial Hospital to see my dad. We arrive around 8:45 a.m. The layout of Mackay is confusing . . . there are so many interconnected buildings and different elevators. It's more chaotic than an airport, but it's still one of the best hospitals in Taipei. I was born in this hospital.

My dad is in the Gospel building, west wing, fourth floor. He occupies the middle bed in a triple room separated by thin, pink curtains. When we arrive, he is resting with a handkerchief over his unblinking eyes to protect them from the harsh fluorescent lighting. His dentures have been removed so his cheeks are hollow, and his mouth remains open in a puckered O. His face is reduced to sharp angles, skin stretched over jutting cheekbones and jaws. He trembles slightly with each breath.

I touch his hand and gently remove the handkerchief and move into his field of vision. "Dad? I'm here. I came back to see you."

His hand is warm, but his whole body is stiff. He stares straight ahead, eyes registering no response. He breathes in and out, in and out. I move closer and continue stroking his hand, struggling to adjust to this new reality.

Un-ho does her best to explain to me in simple Taiwanese what the doctors have been saying. I understand half of what she's telling me. They suspect that my dad has an intestinal obstruction, and he developed pneumonia after arriving at the hospital. The doctor suspended all of his medications including the Parkinson's drugs, which is why he's so stiff. His fever has gone down, and apparently he's better than yesterday. I try to comprehend how this immobile, unresponsive state in which he cannot even recognize his own daughter could be "better" than before.

He is there but not there. I am here, but it is not enough. What was I expecting?

Two nurses come in and work quietly and efficiently on a mobile cart in my dad's shared room. They are grinding up pills with a mortar and pestle. They hand them to Winarti, one of my dad's helpers, and she administers the medicine in a drip to his nose. It's interesting how collaborative the care is. The nurses work side by side with hired domestic helpers, whereas in a US hospital I doubt any non-medical staff would be allowed to help in this way. Mina and Winarti have been here all night. When my relatives arrive to take over the vigil, Mina goes back to Sanhsia to pick up supplies and clean clothes, and Winarti goes out to buy food. I don't know what my family would do without their help.

Each section of the hospital room has a chair that converts to a padded bench for sleeping. Un-ho and I sit side by side on the bench. She is cheerful and talkative and tells me about how she loves cooking but is currently on a special diet for exhaustion and can only eat meat, eggs, bananas, and bamboo shoots. No vegetables, rice, or other fruits. But she still cooks elaborate multi-course meals for her husband and for her grown daughter who still lives at home. Together Un-ho and I figure out how to connect to the hospital Wi-Fi, and then we are released from the burden of small talk through the language barrier, each surrendering to the comforting embrace of our smartphones, the easy escape to anywhere but here.

My Uncle I-to calls Un-ho's phone to talk to me. He says Auntie Huichin will come up from Tainan on Saturday to help. I guess that means he isn't planning on coming himself. I know how busy he is and how much time he has sacrificed to help my family. When my mom suddenly passed away, he and auntie interrupted their vacation in the States where they were visiting their kids and grandchildren so that he could come back to Taiwan to help organize my mom's funeral. He won't say it openly, but I know he is tired of dealing with my family's crises, of being the one to translate and organize and think through all the details—to do what my dad can no longer do.

At 11:30 a.m., Un-ho has to leave the hospital to meet a student for a piano lesson. I'll be on my own for a while. She says goodbye to my dad, but there is no response; he lies there open-mouthed and staring as before.

Tōa-ko·, Un-ho's mother, arrives around twelve thirty. She has visited my dad every day since he was admitted to the hospital, even though she is almost ninety years old and has increasing trouble getting around. Nevertheless, she insists on overseeing her brother's care, and as the matriarch of the Loh family, she is the primary decision maker. I want to say something to express my condolences for her husband, Ko·-tiūⁿ, who passed away earlier this year, but I don't know how.

My stomach is rumbling. I was hoping Tōa-ko· would take me to eat lunch at one of the Japanese restaurants I noticed across from the hospital, but instead she takes out a plastic bag with two steaming sweet potatoes wrapped in paper. At first I say no thanks, but then she offers to split one, so I say yes. She breaks it in half, and we each peel the skin off and eat the creamy orange flesh with our hands. I recall a happier trip many years ago, Anil's first time visiting Taiwan, just a few months after he and I met. My dad had taken him to the outdoor market near the temple, and they bonded over their shared enthusiasm for Taiwanese street food, including roasted sweet potatoes.

These are the sounds I hear at the hospital: Loud coughing and hacking. Light snoring. The violent sound of the curtains between the beds being yanked open or shut. The patient next to the window uttering loud sighs, *Aaaaah!* The occasional gurgle. Mina and Winarti speaking Indonesian to each other. Running water. Toilets flushing. Nurses chatting in Mandarin in the hallway. The *squish-squish* of footsteps in rubber-soled shoes. Slapping sounds when the helpers massage their patrons to improve their circulation while bedridden. Funny ringtones. Wheels on a gurney. Plastic bags rustling. The sound of popping bubbles as Mina plays a game on her cell phone.

The doctor finally comes around 2:20 p.m. He doesn't have much to say. Tōa-ko· explains that the doctor said my dad still has some abdominal/intestinal issues. After the doctor leaves, I go outside for a walk around the hospital. I'm desperate for some fresh air. I walk through the vegetable market and look into restaurant windows to see if there are any good places to eat. On the way back, I stop at the convenience store to buy some Mr.

Brown iced coffee in a can. I know just enough Taiwanese to ask which kind is unsweetened. I go back up to the hospital ward only to discover that everyone is asleep—Tōa-ko· on the foldout bench, my dad in his bed, and Winarti sitting on a stool, slumped over the side of the bed where she had been massaging my dad's hands. There is nowhere for me to sit, so I tiptoe out and find a spot in the waiting area across from radiology.

I pass the time reading articles on my phone. I wish I had brought a book. It's only three thirty. Just a little longer and it will be morning in Oakland, and I can Skype with Anil and Devin—my only real conversation of the day.

Back in the room, Winarti carefully shaves my dad's chin with an electric razor while he's sleeping. She is quietly focused just inches from his face. She is constantly in motion. She's washed him two or three times with a sponge. She gives him medicine and water. She props him up and then lowers him down in the hospital bed. She massages him frequently, puts a handkerchief over his eyes to protect from the harsh light, swabs his lips with water to keep them from getting too dry. I don't know how Winarti does this relentless job and keeps such a good attitude. I'm deeply conflicted about it—grateful for everything she does for my dad but also saddened by the economic realities that force migrants like her to work abroad. She's in her early twenties, still girlish, investing all of her nurturing to care for an old man, my dad, instead of for her own husband and toddler back home in Indonesia. For round-the-clock help and attention, she gets paid the equivalent of US$12,000 per year.

Yesterday, I was in such a hurry to get here. Now I'm here and there is nothing to do except sit and wait, no one to talk to, no family meeting or weighing of treatment options. My dad can't hear me or talk to me, he can't even acknowledge my presence. There is no sudden rebound, no sigh of gratitude and relief that the daughter has come home to settle everything. I flew halfway around the world to be here, but the fact that I am sitting here now breathing the same stale hospital air as my dad changes nothing. There is nothing I can do to help or be useful. In my mind I thought that just the act of coming back would somehow make things better, provide some comfort or reassurance that I was uniquely qualified to give. But now I realize that I am not special. I'm not the wonderful filial daughter who deserves praise for traveling so far and at such expense to be with her dad in what may be his final days. I'm just taking my place among a long line of relatives who are rotating in and out, keeping vigil over my dad, hoping for the slightest improvement, a tiny flicker of recognition and hope.

It's unspoken but clear to me now: I am overdue. I am too little, too late.

The next day, Un-ho and I arrive at the hospital at nine thirty. The doctor came early and we missed him, but there isn't any new information. My dad didn't sleep at all for the second night in a row. He normally takes a sleeping pill, but the doctor took him off all his meds and is slowly adding them back one by one. The Parkinson's medication is the most important, so that is the first to be reintroduced in small doses. Apparently the tranquilizer counteracts the Parkinson's medicine, so temporary sleeplessness is the price for my dad to have a little bit of muscle control and reduced stiffness and tremors.

I go to greet my dad, and although his eyes can't focus on me, he makes a sound when he hears my voice. I sense that he wants to talk, and I lean in closer, but no words come. So I hold his hand and speak to him in a quiet voice for a few minutes, just so he can hear my voice. Although he still can't speak, I feel acknowledged at last.

Later on I hear the sound of light snoring, which makes me

happy. I am relieved my dad is finally able to sleep. It reminds me of a trip several years ago, when I was five months pregnant. At the time, my mom was living at the Suan Lien nursing home, and my dad spent every weekend there with her. Non-residents were not allowed to sleep in the resident's rooms, so my dad and I stayed in the visitor guest rooms, which were like dorms with two single beds. One night, he snored so loud that I could not fall asleep. I was so upset that I took my pillow and blanket and went outside to sleep on the sofa in the communal living room down the hall. But I still couldn't sleep because there was a fly buzzing around that kept me awake. By then I was practically crying from frustration and insomnia. At some point my dad woke up and noticed I wasn't in the room, so he went looking for me. He found me miserably curled up on the sofa and begged me to come back to the room. But today I am grateful to hear my dad snore.

After one day in the hospital, I am now familiar with the delicate ecosystem of this shared space. My dad is in the middle section of a triple room. On his right, in the "window" seat, is an old man who never leaves his bed. The curtain is always drawn so I haven't seen him even once, but I know he is there because of his constant dramatic sighing. *Aaaaah!* A young Indonesian woman, his helper, goes in and out of the room just like Mina and Winarti, buying supplies and food, washing cups in the sink, fetching washcloths, and talking on her cell phone.

On the other side of the room, the "aisle" seat nearest the door, is the patient I call The Gangster. I don't know anything about this man except how he looks and sounds—ruined teeth, smokers rasp, and skin as dark and wrinkled as a raisin. His feet are almost black, suggesting a life of wearing plastic slippers and flip-flops instead of proper shoes with socks. He wears flashy oversized sunglasses in the hospital which is why I call him The Gangster. The card above his bed lists his ailment in English: lung

CA. Un-ho whispers to me that last night he got drunk and wandered around talking to himself, then peed on the floor. Then earlier this morning, he tried to make a run for it. He was arguing with the nurse who was standing in the doorway blocking him and saying he couldn't leave. My relatives are appalled. Tōa-ko· is trying to get my dad transferred to a private room, but the hospital is very crowded. Another one of my cousins works as the resident chaplain, so we are hopeful that through his connections we'll be able to move my dad to more comfortable surroundings.

A group of hospital volunteers comes to sing a few songs for my dad. Judging from the quality of their singing, they must be members of a church choir. There are five of them, and they each hold a hymnbook and sing in perfect harmony. My dad acknowledges them with a sound, trying to say amen and thank you. He is able to see better and move his eyes a little. I can tell he is grateful for their visit, even though he supposedly discourages visitors. Tōa-ko· explained that my dad doesn't want to be seen in this state—immobile, unkempt, unable to speak. At my dad's request, the patient identification placard above his bed does not display his name, just his birth date, patient number, admission date, and provisional diagnosis in English: pneumonia and UGI bleeding. But his attempt to remain incognito isn't working—plenty of visitors seem to find him anyway.

When I come back from a brief walk to get coffee, my dad is sitting up in his bed, trying to talk. I rush to his side and try to listen, but I can't make any sense of his whispered utterings. His mouth is moving and his face strains from the effort of trying to speak. He keeps trying and trying, but all I can hear are indistinct syllables that I cannot interpret. I try repeating certain words to him and guessing what is on his mind. I try going through the alphabet and having him squeeze my finger when I arrive at the right letter, something I had seen in a video, but that doesn't work either. I think I hear him say "I am in pain," or was it "I have to pay," or maybe "I'm near the end?" His face is distorted from the difficulty of trying to express himself. Is he worried about money? Is he worried about paying for the new burial plot my uncle said he bought for himself and my mom? Is he running out of money? I tell him I withdrew most of the funds from the Citibank account, but I don't know if that's what he is worried about. I feel terrible that he's wearing himself out trying to talk, but no one can understand him. He is unreachable.

Tōa-ko· takes me to a Japanese restaurant for dinner. The restaurant is crowded and the service is slow, so by the time we return to the hospital it is after eight o'clock. My dad is again trying to speak, so I lean in closer. I can't make out what he is saying, but he's so insistent; he's sweating and shaking from the effort. Finally I think I hear him say "Teddy" and the names of Ted's children: Jenny, Shelly, and Billy. And then I realize that it is the anniversary of the day my brother passed away four years ago.

Friday morning, I have the idea to ask all of Ted's children to send a video message to Grandpa to cheer him up and reassure him that they are doing okay. I email Jenny and Shelly, and I ask them to forward the request to Billy.

Later, we have a visit from the neurologist, a.k.a. the Parkinson's doctor, or "Pah Keen Son," as everyone says here. Even the doctor refers to himself this way. He examines my dad's tremors which seem worse than yesterday, but it's normal he says. Increasing the Parkinson's medication makes him less rigid but shakier. Decreasing the medicine eases the shaking but makes him stiffer. He asks my dad to open his eyes and to open his mouth, but he can't. This is in stark contrast to the last few days when my dad's eyes and mouth were frozen open and covered with handkerchiefs. Now they are clenched tightly shut and even though he makes a sound to indicate that he can hear the doctor, he isn't able to comply. I can't imagine having so little muscle control that even these small movements are impossible.

The doctor looks at my dad's hands and gently unclenches his fists. When the doctor stops taking notes on his iPad and looks like he is about to leave, I finally get the courage to ask if he speaks English. Yes, he says. I explain that my dad is trying to speak to me but having so much trouble and sweating from the effort. I ask, is he receiving his Parkinson's medication and in the right dose? Would increasing the medication aid his speech? The doctor says he is receiving the full dose although still not taking any of the other medications, and it is best to stay the course and keep observing. He also explains that too high a dose of the Parkinson's medication will cause hallucinations. I nod and thank him.

The lights are turned off for now, and Winarti is playing classical music on her cell phone to help my dad relax. I also play a short video from Devin. I asked him to sing a song for Grandpa and he chose "The Ants Go Marching One by One."

My dad is struggling to tell me something, but I can't understand him, and neither can anyone else. His words are slurred and barely above a whisper, but he keeps trying. Tōa-ko· and I stand close to him, we tell him to relax, to slow down, to try again, but still we only hear vague sounds, not words. It's like he's underwater, his mouth is moving, but the words are carried away by the current, the sound is distorted, the meaning lost.

All my life, my dad's voice was enough for both of us. He was the one who always spoke for me, translated for me, eased my passage across borders, provided the bridge I needed without my having to ask. As the translator's daughter, I was safe, I was accounted for, I never had to worry about being stranded. But what happens when the translator can no longer speak?

Here at the hospital, I'm never alone, but there is no one I can talk to. Tōa-ko· and Un-ho speak Taiwanese to each other and to me. I understand the basics and force myself to speak a little, but it's barely adequate. They speak Mandarin to the hospital staff and the helpers. Mina and Winarti can get by in Mandarin, and they speak to each other in Indonesian. Six people, four languages, but mine is the odd one out, the one that doesn't connect without my dad to link us. My dad is unreachable, unable to help me. I'm an island. I will have to figure out how to get by on my own.

I realize that this is what I fear the most. Not that my dad will die . . . I know it is a real possibility, and yet that doesn't scare me as much. I can't explain it.

What terrifies me is that I will never hear his voice again.

Un-ho now expects me to get to the hospital and return to her apartment on my own. After one day, I have it memorized. From her apartment, turn left at the first corner, then left again at the next alley. I see the OK Mart convenience store and know I'm going the right way when I see the coffee shop on the left. There is a Starbucks at the intersection, and the entrance to the MRT is on the other side. From Shandao Temple Station, I go one stop on the blue line, transfer at Taipei Main Station, and then take the red line two stops north to Shuang Lian. I go out Exit 2 and walk along a tight row of fruit and food stalls on Min Sheng Road. There's another Starbucks and then the intersection with Zhongshan Road and the main entrance to Mackay Memorial Hospital. The whole commute takes about ten minutes.

Today one of my other cousins, Un-liang, comes to visit. She is Un-ho's older sister, the middle one, who works as an ob-gyn. She's short and stout and favors colorful printed batik dresses, which make her resemble one of those nesting Russian dolls. She speaks a little bit of English and is better at translating the medical terms.

A nurse informs us that they found a space on the fourteenth floor and that my dad will be moved to a double room this afternoon. The Gangster is getting discharged, and his friends are packing up his things. He refused all further treatment, against his doctor's orders.

Later we receive a visit from Miss Ho, a young seminary student who visits my dad every week. He calls her his angel. She is standing on one side of my dad's bed, rubbing his arm and humming quietly. He is looking into her eyes. I could be jealous, but I'm not. She has a special relationship with him, and I don't question it. He told me once when he was very sick, right after my mom died, that she prayed for him, and he began to feel better. He was convinced that she had helped him, and he wanted to write about it. Sometimes the people who are the most healing, who have the most profound effect, aren't who you expect.

Bye-bye, 426B. We move to the fourteenth floor, room 1466. It's so much nicer—more spacious, quieter, with better lighting, and not nearly as bustling and chaotic. It's like being upgraded to business class or being promoted from hell to purgatory. Six of us come up with my dad—me, Tōa-ko·, Un-ho, Mina, Winarti, and Miss Ho—prompting the nurse to say, "Are you *all* family?" It's quite an entourage.

My cousin Un-chun (the eldest sister of Un-liang and Un-ho) comes to visit around a quarter to four. She is the one who does the banking for my dad and deals with a lot of his financial paperwork except for any correspondence in English, which she forwards to me. Although I am thankful for her help, she is full of opinions and unsolicited advice and never fails to remind me how much everyone else is doing and how I'm not doing enough.

I'm surprised she waited four days before coming to visit us at the hospital.

The tension of seeing Un-chun is counterbalanced by the joy of seeing my Aunt Emi, who stops by later that afternoon. She's the wife of my mom's youngest brother. I had specifically requested that Tōa-ko· get in touch with her to let her know I was visiting. I had seen Aunt Emi at my mom's funeral the previous summer, but there was no time for an extended visit. That was the first time I had seen my mom's side of the family in years. Aunt Emi had been good friends with my mom, and together they used to be active in feminist groups and activities. Because she spoke English, she always felt like an ally. Years ago we used to visit my Uncle Yoshi and Aunt Emi in Tianmu on a regular basis. My maternal grandmother lived with them too. But once my mom got sick and my dad was consumed with caring for her, he didn't make much of an effort to stay in touch with her side of the family, and we saw them less and less, then not at all.

When Aunt Emi arrives, she goes in to greet my dad, and the look of delight on his face is apparent. He says "Emi!" and I start crying because the recognition is instant, and it is one of the only intelligible things he had said in four days.

After a while, Aunt Emi, Un-chun, and I go out into the hallway to talk privately, and I am quickly overwhelmed. I've spent almost the entirety of the last three days at the hospital. Though I am never alone, there isn't much conversation. But Un-chun has a million things to tell me, including some very complex situations having to deal with my dad's health insurance, his hospital bill from the other hospital, how I need to reestablish my residency in Taiwan, the need to renew my dad's passport, and why they are counseling my dad against selling one of the apartments. One hour of Un-chun talking and Aunt Emi translating is more communication than has happened in the three previous days combined. It is too much for me to take in.

My dad cries whenever the nurse comes into the room because it's usually to suck out the fluid from his lungs and it hurts. The nurse yells in Mandarin, "Grandpa! It's okay! This will only take a moment. You're fine! You're not dying! Don't cry!" She's trying to be friendly and upbeat, but it still scares him.

There's nothing as sad as seeing an old man crying in his hospital bed. It's heartbreaking to see my dad, who was always so mobile and polyglot, now confined to a hospital room, imprisoned by Parkinson's, unable to speak, mumbling incoherently to himself. Is this really what God wanted for him?

An older couple comes to visit my dad at the hospital. I don't know them, but they seem familiar somehow. I apologize for my lousy Taiwanese and to my surprise they speak perfect English, having lived in California for twenty-five years. They are long-time friends of both of my parents; they've known them since we lived at Taiwan Theological Seminary, when I was just a baby. My dad was the dean there, someone everyone looked up to. The woman, who is also named Grace, says she remembers what a shock it was when our family left the seminary suddenly in 1971.

I have a very nice conversation with Grace and Henry, as though they are my old friends rather than people I have just met. When they leave, I feel tears welling up. It's partly the relief of being able to speak English, but it's more than that too. They know who I am without knowing me personally; they have no expectations of me. But they know the overall trajectory of my family, what we've been through, and why I grew up American, basically everything I've been writing about for more than a decade. I feel comforted in the knowledge that for once I don't have to explain myself. They understand. They see in me the small child that was uprooted, not the flawed adult I've become.

What David Bowie Taught Me about Art, Death, and Letting Go

The Montclair Railroad Trail is a mile-long, tree-lined path carved into the side of the Oakland hills. From 1913 until 1957, the trail was part of a passenger rail line that ran from San Francisco through Oakland to Sacramento and Chico. Today it's hard to imagine that trains once rolled on this narrow path through abundant eucalyptus and oak trees; no traces remain of the railroad or the station that once sat at the foot of Paso Robles Drive, an area now occupied by a row of large, immaculate homes with two-car garages and shaded patios.

We go running on the trail almost every week. Years ago I pushed my son Devin in a stroller here; now he runs beside me, and we race the last twenty yards over the footbridge to the stairs that lead to Montclair Village. Every now and then I run alone. I study the trees, and I think about how old they must be, about how they have witnessed so much—the railroad being built then abandoned; houses rising one by one; families arriving, expanding, and eventually leaving to be replaced by new families. Time passes, but the trees always remain, season after season, year after year.

A few weeks ago, we were running on the trail on a Saturday morning. We were nearly at the end and could see the row of houses when I noticed something moving on the ground in front of me. I stopped and shrieked. Devin saw it a split second later and jumped right over it: a thin black snake with a yellow stripe, three or four feet long, whipping back and forth in a violent motion to get across the trail to the grassy slope that led to Shepherd Canyon Road.

It was the first time we had seen a snake on the Montclair trail and the only snake I've ever seen that wasn't eerily slow or still. It felt like an omen, though I was not sure what it meant.

I had just come back from an emergency trip to Taiwan to visit my ailing father, whose health had been declining steadily for more than a year—ever since my mom passed away in July 2014. His main health issue was advanced Parkinson's, and he now lived in a nursing home, but one crisis after another would send him to the hospital on a regular basis—mysterious fevers, blood sugar crashes, digestive problems. The most recent trip was because my dad had developed a serious intestinal blockage caused by a tumor in his pancreas, and the doctors were recommending major surgery that was extremely risky for someone in his frail condition.

My dad's eldest sister and her daughters visited him every week, sometimes daily, and communicated constantly with the nurses, doctors, and my dad's hired caregivers to ensure he received the right treatment. They took in the daily measurements of his blood pressure and blood sugar, how many ounces of his nutritional supplement he received through his feeding tube, and whether he had napped or not. They swabbed his lips with a Q-tip dipped in water to keep his mouth moist. They were on the front lines of caring for my dad in a way that I was not—a chronic source of guilt for me—yet they insisted that any major health care decisions should rest with me. Because of the tumor and recommended surgery, I had been summoned to Taiwan in

March to interpret my dad's final wishes and to sign papers at the hospital either authorizing or declining treatment.

By the time I arrived, the biopsy results were ready. The tumor turned out to be benign, and my dad received a simpler and less invasive laparoscopic procedure to correct the blockage. He had dodged a bullet this time, and I left Taiwan a few days later feeling thankful but still anxious about what was to come.

We returned to the status quo of my dad's slow decline punctuated by occasional visits to the emergency room. Uncle I-to—who is only one year younger than my dad but in much better health—emailed me every few days with updates. My dad's condition was like a roller coaster, careening from stable to critical and back again. The email subject lines say it all: *Update on your dad, Urgent note, He gained more strength now, Good news, To emergency again, Returned, In hospice, Good condition, Be prepared . . .*

I knew deep down, though I didn't want to think about it, that my dad's time was running out. He had just turned eighty-one years old. He was getting weaker and was completely bedridden. He had been in a coma twice, and though he regained consciousness, he was diminished each time. He couldn't read or respond to email as his eyesight was failing. He lacked the strength or motor control to use the iPad we had given him the previous summer. This meant he could no longer continue his projects as a Bible translator, work that kept him happily occupied even though he had officially retired many years ago. We couldn't talk on the phone anymore because his speech was slurred and barely audible. A couple of months ago, my uncle reported that he could no longer speak at all.

A week after I saw the snake on the trail, I had a vivid dream in which I was bitten by a boa constrictor, a large muscular gray snake that could have easily strangled me. I don't recall the setting or what happened right before, but I distinctly remember feeling the snake's fangs piercing my left side and the venom and numbness spreading outward until half of my body was paralyzed. I was scared for a moment, then strangely calm. The world slowed down, stood still.

So this is what it feels like, I thought. *A gentle extinguishing.*

Later that day, I looked up the symbolism of snakes and learned that they are harbingers of change, transformation, and growth. Death and rebirth. Endings and beginnings.

The first week of January 2016, I turned forty-seven. Three days later, David Bowie released his final album, *Blackstar,* and two days after that, he succumbed to liver cancer. I had not been a huge Bowie fan, but I was swept up in the massive worldwide outpouring of grief for a beloved and iconic musician. It quickly became apparent that he had known the end was coming; *Blackstar* was threaded with references to his own mortality.

One of my Facebook friends reacted to the news of his death with this simple, perfect statement: MAKE ART, DON'T WAIT. It was an appeal to those of us who create—but don't necessarily make a living at it—to work harder to realize our artistic ambitions. In other words, our time on earth is finite . . . don't die with unfinished business . . . make the art that only you can make.

This epiphany was powerfully reinforced just a few months later when Prince passed away at the age of fifty-seven, less than two months after he had performed at an arena show in the Bay Area. A few of my friends had attended that show; none of them suspected that that would be one of his last concerts. The impact on my generation—on those of us who grew up with *Purple Rain* as our high school soundtrack—was seismic. My friends and I traded stories about our Prince memories, like when I was sixteen and went to Paris on a summer exchange program and bought myself a raspberry beret. Losing Prince felt personal, like losing a part of my childhood.

Prince and Bowie weren't especially linked in life, but they were connected by the proximity of their untimely deaths and also by their artful, uninhibited style and gender-bending sensibility. I didn't have any Prince albums on my iPod, but I had a David Bowie compilation that I started listening to over and over in my car. I read countless articles about both artists in the days following their deaths. One particular quote stayed with me, which had been posted on Twitter: *So David Bowie was the scout team and he sent word to Prince once he had found a new acceptable planet.* This seemed so perfect to me, to imagine them not dead but reunited somewhere in outer space, cosmic roommates searching for a groovy new place to call home.

Around this time, my son Devin developed a keen interest in architecture. We had traveled to Los Angeles earlier in the year and visited the huge Frank Gehry retrospective at the Los Angeles County Museum of Art. We had given Devin a digital camera the previous Christmas, and this was the first time he had used it. He was enthralled by the Gehry scale models of architectural projects from all over the world and took so many photos that I had to admonish him: "You don't need a picture of every single thing!" But he was not deterred. Between the Gehry exhibit, another modern art exhibit at LACMA, and the beautiful gardens at the Getty Center, Devin took more than 200 photos over two days.

A few weeks later, I took Devin to the newly reopened Berkeley Art Museum and Pacific Film Archive in downtown Berkeley, where we saw an exhibit called *Architecture of Life*. We explored the galleries and enjoyed the building itself, which was full of unique vantage points and unexpected details, like the all-red stairwells. But the work that riveted us the most was a huge mural at the entrance called *The World Garden* by Qiu Zhijie.

The World Garden is a large fictional map done in the style of classical Chinese landscape painting, with dramatic rocky peaks, delicate pagodas, and mist-shrouded trees and waterfalls. Labels in English and Chinese denote landmarks of interest, such as the Moon Worshipping Pavilion and Garden of Reciprocal Enlightenment. While many of the names conform to the quaint, poetic turns of phrase we expect from English translations of Chinese, some subvert our expectations by making an explicit double entendre (Sexual Desire in Spring) while others sound simply awkward in translation (Modesty and Politeness of Water). My favorites were the place names that described reflective, melancholy states of mind such as The Lake of Lonely Happiness and The More Beautiful the Scenery the More Despair the Heart.

The irony is that this monumental landscape, depicting scenery that's meant to endure, is actually temporary. The Art Wall in the front of BAMPFA is designed to be painted over every few months with the work of a new artist.

A few weeks after our visit, Devin said to me out of the blue: "When I grow up, I want to be an artist inspired by space, science, and architecture."

I was thrilled. Anil and I have been trying to encourage his interest and abilities in the arts, sciences, and music. He's been taking electric guitar lessons. He performs in a band with other eight-year-olds and has already composed one song. We take him to concerts and museums as much as we can. I want him to know that there's more to life than sports, TV, and video games. I want Devin to appreciate literature, art, music, and architecture because they have the ability to endure, to connect us to past and future generations. Exposing him to these influences is my way of saying to him: *Make art. Make music. Create or discover some-*

thing that outlives you. Work on something that will have meaning long after you are gone. Just like your Grandpa did.

For weeks and weeks, I listened to the David Bowie album on repeat in my car. I thought about the snakes, the prophesy of change, and the metaphor of space. There were almost too many space references to count: "Ashes to Ashes," "Ziggy Stardust," "Starman," "Life on Mars?" And, of course, the song "Changes." But more than anything I became obsessed with "Space Oddity." Even Devin, who was often in the car with me, would listen reverently and beg me to turn up the volume whenever it came on. We memorized the lyrics.

"Space Oddity" was released in 1969, the year I was born and the year of the first moon landing. At the time, audiences thought the song was inspired by Apollo 11 since the song came out the same week. Others have theorized that the troubled character of Major Tom was an avatar for a seriously drug-addicted Bowie, whose losing contact with Ground Control and floating into outer space was a metaphor for an overdose.

For me it took on another meaning. I thought about my dad, lying in his hospital bed, waiting to be liberated from a body that was failing him. He was fitted with tubes for breathing, eating, and eliminating. He could no longer sit or stand, write or speak: this man who used to be so mobile, who circled the globe so many times, who made an art of translating and communicating. His purpose in life had been to help others, and now he himself was helpless. Although he never said it to me, I can't imagine he thought of his wrecked, aging body as anything other than a prison.

But still, he hung on for months. And we hung on to him.

The more I listened to "Space Oddity," the more it took on a talismanic quality. I held onto it the way one holds onto a charm, certain that I needed it even though I could not explain why.

The song, I finally realized, was telling us both to let go. To not be afraid.

This is Major Tom to Ground Control
I'm stepping through the door
And I'm floating in a most peculiar way.

The Sunday before I was to travel to Taiwan again, we went running on the trail. Devin was going to a *Star Wars* birthday party in the afternoon, and I reminded him to make a card for his friend. As an afterthought, I asked if he could make a nice card for Grandpa too.

"What should I say?" he asked. "Get well soon?"

"No," I said, choking up.

"Why not?"

I took a deep breath.

"Grandpa isn't going to get better," I said.

We paused in front of our house so that I could break off a sprig of rosemary for our lunch. We each inhaled the sharp green smell and sighed. Devin leaned into me, and I put my arm around him.

"Is Grandpa dying?" His eyes searched mine.

"Yes," I finally said, "but we don't know when. That's why I have to go visit him now."

I'm not sure who said it first, but this quote resonates with me today: "We are all made of the dust of exploding stars." We are interconnected; we are the universe, and the universe is us. In this way, the past touches the future and everything in between.

Maybe, I think, dying is not the end but just another change, a journey to somewhere unknown but ultimately peaceful.

Only two months after my previous trip, I went to visit my dad again for five days in Taiwan. He had been transferred to hospice a few weeks earlier. The staff had advised my relatives that we should invite close friends and family to visit him and say goodbye while we could. We held a small gathering on Wednesday evening, where his longtime Bible translation colleagues took turns telling stories about him and thanking him for his mentorship, and we all sang my dad's favorite hymns, including a few he composed himself. I organized a four-way video call with the grandchildren, who were in three different time zones: New York, London, and Bangkok. (It was the middle of the night in California, so Devin could not participate.) We all chatted with my dad and gave him updates on our lives, but none of us said an official "goodbye."

On my final day in Taiwan, I visited my dad one last time. I did not know what to say. In my heart I knew this might be our last conversation, but I could not find the right words.

What I ended up saying was: "I'll take care of everything," meaning I would make sure any money left in his estate went to support the education of his grandchildren. This was his one remaining concern, and I wanted him to know that I would carry out his wishes.

Since he was lying on a hospital bed, his arms stiff at his side, I couldn't hug him properly. So instead I laid my head gently on his chest, and I felt him inhale and exhale a few times. His breathing was steady and surprisingly vigorous.

"Bye, Dad. I love you." And then it was time to go.

Sixteen hours later, I landed at SFO. I texted Anil to let him know I'd arrived, then I started downloading my email messages on my phone. Scrolling quickly through them, my eye landed on a note from my cousin Leng that said *I just heard the news. I'm so sorry.*

What news? I thought to myself, then . . . *Oh no. No!*

I was standing in the airport immigration line with hundreds of people trudging one step at a time toward passport control when I saw the email from my uncle saying my dad had passed away. It took a few minutes for the news to sink in.

I realized that my dad waited to let go until he knew I was safely on my way. He took care of me first, just like he always did.

On the last Friday in May, my dad and I both flew home.

Double Life

On March 19, 2017, I was surprised to see a Facebook notification that Milo Thornberry had accepted my friend request. Two nights before, I had read Milo's obituary in the *Bend Bulletin,* an Oregon newspaper. He passed away on March 8, at the age of seventy-nine.

I had sent the request several months before, when Milo commented on a photo I posted about my dad's passing and memorial service from earlier that summer. Milo and his then-wife Judith were close friends with my parents when we lived at Taiwan Theological Seminary in Taipei from 1968 to 1971. They were American missionaries on the faculty of the seminary, and my dad was the dean. Their young daughter Elizabeth was my brother Ted's earliest playmate.

Scrolling through Milo's timeline, I figured out that the most recent activity—including the friend acceptance—had been posted by his son, Richard. The last time Richard and I saw each other was sometime in the 1970s, when his family visited mine in New Jersey. I have a blurry snapshot of five kids lined up behind a birthday cake: Elizabeth and Ted in the back row in their early teenage years, and the younger kids—Katy, Richard, and me—in the front row. I look about eight years old. My guess is confirmed by the eight candles on the cake.

Earlier black-and-white photos from the seminary show Ted and Elizabeth squeezed together on a single swing, legs akimbo, smiling and laughing. Another shows Ted on a large tricycle with Elizabeth standing on his right side. In front, balanced on the handlebars by a woman I don't recognize, is a six-month-old baby with a serious expression: me.

Richard and I were so young that these photos stand in for any actual memories we might have of each other. What I do recall is that his dark hair and Asian face made him look more like Ted and me than his blonde sisters, Elizabeth and Katy.

Richard's family forever changed the life of my family. I wonder if he remembers?

Of course he remembers.

Milo wrote a memoir called *Fireproof Moth: A Missionary in Taiwan's White Terror,* published in 2011, about his involvement in a clandestine mission that changed the course of Taiwanese history. The book describes his relationship with Peng Ming-min, a prominent Taiwanese activist and dissident.

Peng was a professor of law and political science when the Kuomintang recruited him to advise the Republic of China delegation to the United Nations. He became disillusioned with the abuses of Chiang Kai-shek's regime during martial law and the White Terror, and he secretly wrote a manifesto calling for Chiang to be ousted and for Taiwan to become democratic and declare independence. Peng was imprisoned in 1965, then due to public pressure from Amnesty International among others, he was released to house arrest where he was under constant surveillance by the KMT.

During this time, Peng met Milo and Judith, who became sympathetic to his cause. He visited them from time to time at the seminary, trailed by KMT agents. Although Milo and Judith had no political or diplomatic experience, they joined a loose con-

sortium of friends and activists who collaborated to help Peng
escape to freedom. They had one key advantage: as foreigners
they flew under the radar of the KMT security forces.

My mom met the famous dissident only once. One day Judith
offered her a ride down the mountain to go to the market. When
she got into the car, she was startled to see Peng sitting in the
backseat. Judith introduced the two of them, but after saying
hello, my mom was speechless for the rest of the fifteen-min-
ute ride. She was starstruck but also afraid: although Peng was
a hero among Taiwanese people, his presence was toxic. As a
known enemy of the government, being associated with him was
extremely risky. Everyone knew what the KMT was capable of
during Chiang's dictatorship.

On January 2, 1970, in the quiet lull after new year celebrations, three families went about their routines. My parents were
preparing to celebrate my first birthday, unaware that their
friends were leading a double life. Across the street, Milo and
Judith tended to their adopted newborn son, Richard, who was
finally starting to gain weight and thrive. The call from the adoption agency had come at the worst possible time, in the middle
of delicate preparations to help Peng flee the country, but they
did not hesitate to say yes. Peng gave the baby the Chinese name
Tang Chih-min, meaning "intelligent, wise leader." That night, in
the final hours before the plan was set into motion, there was
nothing more Milo and Judith could do except pray.

Peng, who had been staying with friends, slipped into his
home one last time after midnight. He tiptoed into the bedrooms
where his wife, son, and daughter slept and bid them a silent
goodbye, unsure of when or if he would see them again. They
knew nothing about the plan or the great danger that awaited
him in the next twenty-four hours. This was for their own safety.
In advance he had prepared two media statements: one that

would be published if he was captured or killed, and one that would be used if he managed to escape.

The next day, aided by an elaborate disguise, fake passport, and a network of volunteers at various checkpoints along the way, Peng boarded a flight for Hong Kong and eventually landed in Sweden where he was granted asylum. His dramatic escape made headlines around the world and was a major embarrassment for Chiang and the KMT.

A seemingly impossible goal had been achieved, but the impact continued to reverberate in Taiwan. One year later, Milo and his family were surrounded and detained by KMT security forces at their house at the seminary. My parents closed the curtains and watched nervously from the window. Two days after that, Milo's family was deported back to the US, and their passports were revoked without explanation, putting an end to their missionary work overseas.

Although my parents were not involved in the plan, their friendship with Milo and Judith put them at risk. They were being watched by the KMT, and they heard a rumor that they had been blacklisted. Then, miraculously, my dad was offered a job in New York, which he immediately accepted. I was two years old when we left.

Fast forward two decades . . . Martial law was lifted, and Taiwan eventually became democratic. After more than twenty years in exile, Peng returned to a hero's welcome. In 1995 he ran for president in Taiwan's first democratic election.

My parents also returned home after almost twenty years abroad, but it was too late for my brother and me. Our exile lasted so long that Ted and I were forever changed. We grew up American by accident, wayward seeds on distant shores.

And now here I am reconnecting with Milo's children on Facebook, decades after the dramatic events that upended our lives.

I think again of those old black-and-white photos, and I wonder: *Does my lost childhood exist in the pages of their albums, just as theirs exists in mine? Does Richard feel the same sense of loss and rootlessness, and carry the same scars of that violent separation from our homeland?*

I send him a friend request and wait for a sign.

Mooncake

Normally I am the first to wake up on Saturdays, but today I was the last. I sensed my husband getting out of bed and the cat stretching and repositioning herself in the warm spot he left behind. I felt heavy and immobile. Was it because of the glass of wine I drank last night? I rolled over on my side to face the window, eyes still shut. The last wisps of a dream came back to me, and I realized I wasn't ready to leave.

I dreamed that I saw my parents. We were sitting at a round table inside a windowless dining room. My dad sat across from me, my mom at his right side. Someone whose face I couldn't see sat in between me and her, and there was another person on my right, in between me and my dad, who might have been his younger brother, my Uncle I-to. There were round white plates on the table but no silverware or napkins. In front of my dad was something flat and yellow on a plate—a dried radish omelet, a Taiwanese specialty. On top of it was a single, small round pastry which I recognized as a mooncake.

We are quiet around the table. My dad is cutting the omelet and mooncake into four pieces even though there are five of us. The only words I hear are my dad muttering, "I haven't even served this yet, and already more food is arriving." He is looking over my shoulder, at someone I cannot see approaching the table with more food.

That's all I remember of the dream. What does it mean?

I compare it to other dreams. Whenever I dream about my parents, they are middle-aged, in their fifties or sixties, before disease and old age have taken their toll. The setting is usually flat and austere like a stage set, devoid of extraneous details or bright colors. I think of the paintings of Zhang Xiaogang, which depict parents and children in shades of gray, always facing forward, never smiling. The only sensory things I can recall are the white of the plates, the yellow omelet, the golden-brown mooncake.

I've never been fond of mooncakes. Although they are beautiful to look at, the traditional fillings of sweet red bean, lotus seed paste, and egg yolks don't appeal to me. I didn't enjoy such types of sweet, starchy desserts partly because my dad was diabetic and partly because living in America had prejudiced my palate; my idea of sweets was limited to chocolate, vanilla, and fruit flavors. But now I feel a strange nostalgia for mooncakes because of what they symbolize: family reunions, sharing, the togetherness of many generations. This seasonal delicacy that I rejected in my youth has come to symbolize what I've lost.

It's been thirty years since I lived under the same roof—or in the same country—as my parents. My mom passed away first, six years ago, then my dad two years ago. There is no one left who will think of me during Mid-Autumn Festival.

I suddenly remember all the prohibitions against sharing food with the dead. In the movie *Spirited Away*, Chihiro's parents are lured by the smell of cooked meat into a lively night market that is populated with feasting hungry ghosts. They eat their fill and are turned into animal spirits. When Persephone is kidnapped by Hades, he tricks her into eating pomegranate seeds in the underworld, and thereafter she is doomed to return there annually, causing the earth above to become cold and barren and devoid of crops each winter. In the Sumerian myth of Inanna, her faithful servant, Ninshubur, leads a rescue party to bring her back from the underworld, where she has gone to visit her sister, Queen Ereshkigal. The rescuers are given strict instructions by Enki not to eat or drink anything during their mission.

It's common in many religions and belief systems to leave offerings of food and drink for the dead. When the living offer food to the dead, there's no issue. But do the opposite and you risk severe punishment; the living must not consume the food of the dead.

In the dream, I am not the one serving food. My dad is serving us. The more I think about it, the more questions I have. Is this the past, present, or future? Are my parents living or dead? Who are the other guests? Why is my dad cutting the omelet and mooncake into four portions and not five? Is there someone among us who is a ghost? Or are all of them ghosts except me?

Who is it that is not counted? What will happen if I take a bite?

Feathers from Home and Other Family Heirlooms

For a long time, I had only one memory of my great-grandmother, A-tso. It wasn't a happy one. So, I was intrigued when my Auntie Huichin recently told me a story I'd never heard about A-tso—doubling the knowledge I had about the oldest relative I'd ever met—just a few weeks after my dad passed away.

We had completed a whirlwind of family events in my dad's honor: the viewing, cremation, memorial service, and placement of the urn in its final resting place in the columbarium next to my mom's ashes. In the first forty-eight hours I was in Taiwan, I had not been alone for a single minute; I went from shaking hands and accepting condolences from dozens of relatives and friends to attending a somber family meeting in order to decide how to divide my dad's estate, to smiling through a formal dinner with my dad's Bible translation colleagues while pretending to enjoy sea cucumber and abalone. We had one day to relax before all of the out-of-town family members returned home.

After being constantly surrounded by people for three days, I was suddenly alone. Without all the buzz and activity to distract me, all the feelings I had been trying to avoid flooded in; I felt untethered and off balance, trapped in a strange world where everything looked familiar but nothing was the same. I was a child without parents, a tree without roots.

For the first time, I was left to navigate my way around Taiwan without any parental help. After my husband and son returned to California, I checked out of the hotel in Taipei and went to stay at my parents' ninth floor apartment in Sanhsia with the goal of sorting through a lifetime's worth of their belongings. It was after five o'clock when I arrived during a lull in the heavy downpour that struck almost every afternoon. I opened the door with my key and entered the apartment like I had hundreds of times before, only this time there was no one to greet me.

The apartment was piled high with cardboard boxes, a result of my dad selling the fourth-floor apartment a year ago and consolidating their things in the one property he still owned. It was dusty, claustrophobic, and hopelessly cluttered, more like a storage unit than a place where someone had actually lived. On previous trips I had managed to poach Wi-Fi from a neighbor, but now all the networks were password protected. I couldn't get the TV or the stereo to work. There was no dial tone when I picked up the telephone. It scared me a little, being so completely cut off from the outside world in that apartment. All the noise and energy that used to fill this space—conversations with my mom and dad, an endless loop of Taiwanese TV news, the hiss of vegetables being stir-fried in a wok, the chirping sound of the doorbell when we had visitors—was gone, replaced by stale air and an unsettling quiet. I felt like I had crossed a threshold into a forbidden place, like Dante in purgatory, a tourist in the land of the dead. Eventually I managed to get over my uneasiness and fall asleep on the living room sofa; I could not bring myself to sleep in my dad's bed.

The following day, Auntie Huichin arrived from Tainan to help me clean out the apartment. She and my Uncle I-to had also gone to graduate school in the US in the 1960s and partially raised their three children there. Auntie and Uncle speak English fluently, and their experiences mirrored my own parents' in many ways. After my dad became incapacitated a couple of years ago, they were the ones who translated for me and passed on any news from our Taiwanese relatives.

Auntie Huichin is a no-nonsense kind of person; she immediately went to work sorting through the boxes, bookshelves, and closets in the bedrooms, while I did the same in the living room. Every now and then I would pause to ask her a question or show her an old black-and-white photo I'd discovered. Or she would come to the living room holding some object and say, "Look what I found. Do you want to keep it?" The first time she said that, she had found a brittle plastic folder with the original life insurance policy my mom had purchased for my dad more than forty years ago—an account I had been trying unsuccessfully to cash out for years. A couple of hours later, she again emerged from the bedroom and said, "Grace, look at this!"

She held up a small feather duster and a big smile spread across her face. I'm sure I looked thoroughly confused. "Maybe you did not know this," she said, "but A-tso used to make these feather dusters by hand. This looks like one of hers. I think you should keep it."

She went on to describe how my A-tso—her husband's grandmother—had come to her on the eve of her departure for New York, where she was planning to join my Uncle I-to at Union Theological Seminary. A-tso said to her, "I have something for you," while making a show of concealing something behind her back. The implication was that it was a special memento of some sort, perhaps an heirloom she would be entrusted with.

A-tso revealed the gift she'd brought: a handmade feather duster made with chicken feathers. A-tso was very proud of the feather dusters and considered herself an artisan of sorts. She painstakingly collected the feathers, arranged them carefully by size and color so they formed a perfect spray, and then tied them with thread onto a stick that was only slightly bigger than a chopstick. This was her art, and she had bestowed one of these specimens on her grandson's wife, who was about to travel overseas to meet him.

Auntie Huichin said A-tso probably did the same thing for my mom when she left Taiwan to go to Princeton, New Jersey. My mom had gone earlier than my dad, and they weren't married yet. I tried to imagine how my mom would have reacted more than fifty years ago to A-tso's gift. Did she hide her disappointment, having expected a more lavish or romantic gift as the fiancée of the favorite son? Or was she delighted and grateful to receive something that was not only handmade but also lightweight and practical? A generation ago this might have been special, but to me it seemed rather boring and mundane . . . even backward. Would I really keep such a thing?

I tried to reconcile this vision of A-tso as a sort of fairy godmother to her granddaughters-in-law with the stern, hunched old lady I met the first time we went back to Taiwan after living in the States. I was nine years old the summer we visited on the way to Hong Kong, where my dad had been transferred for work. By then I was a thoroughly American kid who only spoke English and felt profoundly out of place in Taiwan.

My single encounter with A-tso was the most dramatic example of that. When we visited the compound—the home of several generations of the Loh family in Sanhsia—I was taken to an outdoor courtyard, where a tiny old lady was sitting on a stool. She wore a baggy black tunic and pants, and her thin hair was pulled back in a tight bun.

My dad nudged me forward to greet her. She looked me up and down, noticing my long, ponytailed hair—well past shoulder length, in contrast with the chin-length bobs of all the Taiwanese schoolgirls we had seen—and my shorts, which at that time were not worn by girls in Taiwan. Her mouth twisted into a scowl.

"Is this a boy or a girl?" she demanded. "Maybe I should pull down the pants to see for sure!"

I didn't understand what she had said, but I was stung by her obvious disapproval. I was scared of her after that, and I always felt ashamed in her presence.

Now here I was nearly four decades later, holding something A-tso had made before I was even born—something created out of affection, pride, and the desire to send a memento of Taiwan with the granddaughters who were leaving for a new life far away. Maybe A-tso thought the feather duster would protect them, like a talisman, prevent them from losing their Taiwanese-ness—from turning into foreign devils like me.

Taiwan was under martial law then, and it was rare for Taiwanese people to travel outside the country unless, like my parents, they were students who had been admitted to foreign universities. Back then, the flight from Taiwan to California took nearly a full day with two stops in between, and then it took another half-day to reach New York. Those who were lucky enough to go abroad did so with no guarantee of when they would be able to return home. There was no easy, instant communication through email, Skype, or social media; you couldn't beam yourself into someone's living room from halfway across the world or watch videos of the weddings and other family events you missed because you lived in another country.

Telephones were a relative luxury owned by a handful of families, and even if you did have one, long-distance phone calls were expensive and required the assistance of a live telephone operator. The majority of person-to-person communication was conducted through handwritten letters. Urgent messages were conveyed by telegram. Ordinary news traveled by surface mail, which took a month or longer, or by airmail using the thinnest onionskin paper or aerogrammes with an accelerated delivery schedule of two weeks.

You were lucky to have one decent photo of a loved one that you could bring with you overseas as cameras were still mostly owned and used by professionals; photography for the masses was still years away. Photos were precious, physical objects that existed in finite quantities, unlike the endless proliferation of digital images we have today. Because of the difficulty of communication and limited ability to travel home, whatever you put in your suitcase to bring with you was incredibly important. If you wanted to remember someone or something, you had to choose carefully.

I imagine my mom, or my Auntie Huichin, selecting what to bring with them on a trip halfway across the world. Clothes for all kinds of weather; a few family photographs; a ring or a necklace given to them by their mothers; two or three books; their best shoes; an address book with contact information for all their relatives in Taiwan, plus a few friends-of-friends to look up in the tri-state area; a handheld mirror; a purse. There wasn't room for anything frivolous.

Under these circumstances, maybe A-tso's feather duster was the perfect gift after all. *Don't forget your parents,* it said. *Don't forget the labor of those who helped you succeed. Don't forget these mountains, this landscape. Etch them into your mind so that Taiwan never leaves you.*

Today, the feather duster might not make it through customs. But fifty years ago, it was an ideal souvenir, the closest one could get to bringing back actual Taiwanese soil—a tangible reminder of the land and life my mom and my aunt were leaving behind. I faced the same decision that day in my parents' apartment, when Auntie Huichin told me the story of A-tso's feather dusters: What, if anything, would make it into my suitcase as a piece of Taiwan and my parents that I could bring home with me?

In the end, I didn't take the feather duster. I asked Auntie Huichin to organize an open house for our relatives to take whatever they wanted of my parents' leftover possessions—clothes, books, furniture, dishes, and more. I knew they would claim everything that was usable and practical.

I, on the other hand, did not want anything useful. Instead I sought out objects that had deep personal significance—things that represented what my parents had loved and what I loved about them. My mom had been a museum lover and art history professor with a PhD in Japanese literature, so I chose a set of art postcards showing famous scenes from *The Tale of Genji* to remind me of her. My dad, who raised me in a houseful of books, had been a scholar and translator also known for his collection of more than one hundred water buffalos, a symbol of the hardworking Taiwanese and their agricultural roots. I picked one of his favorites to take home, a smooth wooden sculpture with a mother and calf in a tender pose, set on a base the shape of a leaf—the shape of Taiwan.

Uncertain Ground

In October 2018, I noticed my Taiwanese and Chinese American friends posting photos of large family gatherings and mooncakes. Others posted photos of visiting the graves of family members. I felt a wave of panic and guilt. Had I missed Tomb Sweeping Day, when I should have been honoring my deceased parents? On the other hand, I remembered and looked forward to Dia de los Muertos, a holiday I hadn't grown up with but learned about by living in California for more than twenty years. How could I feel such a strong affinity for a Mexican cultural tradition while being so ignorant of the holidays observed by the Taiwanese and Chinese diaspora?

A quick Wikipedia search revealed that I had gotten my holidays mixed up. Mid-Autumn Festival celebrates the full moon at harvest time, with families reuniting for a traditional feast and mooncakes. Tomb Sweeping Day (Qing Ming) is one of several holidays to remember your ancestors, but it's observed in spring. I could not remember which was which because my family did not really celebrate these holidays. Although I was born in Taiwan, I spent my early childhood in New Jersey, and then from fourth grade through high school graduation, we lived in Hong Kong.

We were a curious cultural hybrid: a family of Taiwanese origin living as American expatriates in a British territory where we resembled the local Chinese population but did not speak the same language and had little in common with them. I attended an American school full of American and international students. One of the advantages of attending Hong Kong International School was that we got American, British, *and* Chinese holidays off: Thanksgiving, the Queen's Birthday, and Lunar New Year.

I'm sure we learned about Mid-Autumn Festival and Qing Ming, but they weren't as memorable as Lunar New Year, the biggest holiday of the year, when everyone got a week off from school or work. Children and younger relatives received lai see (hong bao), red envelopes filled with spending money, and employees received their annual bonuses. I remember going with my parents to join the enormous crowds down in Causeway Bay, pushing for a spot close to the harbor to get the best view of the spectacular fireworks. Stores and restaurants tried to outdo each other with elaborate "Kung Hei Fat Choy" decorations and special menus and promotions. Everywhere you went, people were in a festive good mood.

Since we did not have any relatives in Hong Kong, there were no family obligations during Lunar New Year. It was only the four of us—my mom, my dad, Ted, and me—so at most we would go out for a fancy restaurant meal. We did not go from house to house with bottles of Johnnie Walker or baskets of tangerines. We did not make hundreds of homemade dumplings or go to the bank to request a wad of crisp new bills to stuff into red envelopes for my younger cousins, nieces, and nephews. My parents might have hung up modest decorations outside our apartment door, but I think it was just for show, so we would not appear strange to our neighbors.

Once I asked my parents why we didn't do more to celebrate

the Taiwanese and Chinese holidays. "Well," my dad said, "it's because we are Christian. From when we were little, we only celebrated Christmas and Easter. Your grandpa was very strict. We were forbidden from observing any of the non-Christian, Taiwanese traditions because that was considered superstitious."

I was relieved that my ignorance was not my fault. But I still felt a void.

When we moved from New Jersey to Hong Kong in the summer of 1978, we visited Taiwan for the first time in seven years. I was only two years old when we left in 1971, so I had no real memories of my birthplace. Everything was strange and new—the crowds, the unfamiliar food, the damp heat and smells of Taipei, and the sudden immersion in a language I barely knew, like being neck-deep in water without knowing how to swim. My relatives were shocked that I could not speak Taiwanese, though I understood a little, so they spoke in the loud, exaggerated tone reserved for preschoolers. *How old are you? Are you hungry? Do you like Taiwan?*

The summer went by in a blur of family visits. I spent a lot of time sitting quietly beside my parents; eating from trays of mango and guava; and reading comic books while they talked for hours with my aunts and uncles, catching up on everything they had missed during their years abroad. My cousins made half-hearted attempts to play with me, but they quickly gave up; I was too weird, too alien. In the late seventies there were hardly any "foreign ghosts" in Taiwan, so I was seen as an aberration—not as someone who spoke another language but someone who could not speak at all. I looked like everyone else but suffered from an invisible defect that made me incomplete.

While I wrestled with culture shock, my parents were

relieved to finally be home after seven years. More than anything, my mom regretted not returning for her father's funeral when he passed away in 1975. It was too expensive and all but impossible with two young children to raise while my dad worked. I did not realize until I was much older that the real reason my mom didn't go back was the fear that had caused them to leave in the first place. My parents didn't dare return to Taiwan until after we had naturalized as US citizens and had the protection of our crisp, dark blue, eagle-embossed American passports.

One of my earliest memories is of being taken to the main library at Princeton. I must have been three or four years old. I felt very small, dwarfed by the floor-to-ceiling bookcases of rare and unusual books. My dad led me to a corner of the library where there was a large standing globe. It was taller than I was. He spun it around, located a small, sweet-potato shaped island off the southeastern coast of China, and said to me: "That's where you were born." The speck on the globe was labeled Formosa, dubbed "the beautiful island" by Portuguese explorers. Taiwan was no more than an idea to me at the time, so he did his best to make it tangible.

At that age, I didn't distinguish between the many countries in Asia, and I felt a sort of compulsory kinship with anyone who looked like me, even if they weren't Taiwanese. One summer, a Chinese kid named Herman was the driver of our neighborhood ice cream truck. He was probably sixteen or seventeen years old, with an overgrown bowl cut and glasses; he looked like an older version of my brother, Ted. I used to tell people Herman was my cousin; it seemed plausible back then that anyone who looked Asian could be related to us.

I remember clearly my few instances of exposure to Asian cultures when we lived in New Jersey, which I can fit into one paragraph. In New York's Chinatown we used to buy sweet noodle cakes, dried cuttlefish, pastel colored shrimp chips, and other exotic snacks. Once or twice a year we'd have dinner at a fancy Japanese restaurant where the grownups ate raw fish, fried food, and weird pickles while I refused everything except a steaming bowl of udon. I remember my mom obsessively watching TV news about the trial of the Gang of Four after the flameout of the Chinese Cultural Revolution, and I remember our whole family gathering in front of our black-and-white TV to watch a lengthy film adaptation of Gilbert & Sullivan's *The Mikado* starring white actors in yellowface, a memory that now makes me cringe.

It took me a long time to realize my family didn't fit the typical immigrant narrative. We didn't settle down permanently in the US nor did we sponsor and bring over a large clan of relatives. But we weren't alone either. We were part of a tight-knit Taiwanese American community that went to church, barbecues, and birthday parties together.

All that changed when we moved to Hong Kong. There we were surrounded by Chinese and Asian cultures, although we experienced it inside of an expat bubble. My dad's colleagues were Korean, Indonesian, Australian, Indian, and British, in addition to locals from Hong Kong. We did not know any other Taiwanese families in Hong Kong but visited our own relatives in Taiwan at least once a year. We had the illusion of proximity: Taipei and Hong Kong are only one and a half hours apart by plane. Our cities lit up simultaneously with Lunar New Year celebrations and suffered damage and destruction from the same typhoons. But in retrospect, I think my parents were lonely. Although geographically close, we were further isolated from Taiwan.

Moving to Hong Kong flipped my identity to its inverse, like a film negative: I went from being a racial outsider and linguistic insider in New Jersey to being a racial insider and linguistic outsider in Hong Kong and Taiwan. Either way, I was a misfit; I was always disappointing someone, always falling short.

My first close encounter with death was when I was twelve years old.

When we lived in Hong Kong, every Sunday we took two forms of public transportation—a minibus and the brand-new MTR subway system—across the harbor to attend Kowloon Union Church. KUC had an international congregation of people from all over the world attending worship services in English.

Like Hong Kong itself, KUC was a revolving door of expats who came and went, rarely staying for more than a few years at a time. But I looked forward to Sundays because I got to see my best friend, Frances, who was from Switzerland. Although we were the same age, we attended different schools. Her father was a chef at a high-end hotel, and her mother was an artist. I remember being very impressed that Frances was fluent in French and English. She had gorgeous wavy brown hair and a mole above her lip; she was destined to be a beautiful young woman.

Frances and I used to hang out after church and go shopping, just the two of us, along the busy retail district on Nathan Road known as the Golden Mile. We'd go to gift and stationery stores and buy Hello Kitty trinkets, or we'd go to the Yue Hwa China Products store and buy black cloth Mary Janes or embroidered satin pouches. At age twelve, we didn't have a lot to spend, but we had ample time to explore and enjoy our first taste of freedom away from our parents. They trusted us as long as we stuck together and came home by four or five o'clock in the afternoon.

In Hong Kong, we had to get used to using a gas burner for cooking and heating water. My parents taught me how to turn on the pilot light on the stove and how to turn on the gas water heater in the bathroom. They instructed me to always remember to prop open the narrow bathroom window whenever I took a bath or a shower.

One evening after dinner, my dad received a phone call from Frances's father. I was doing homework in my bedroom, so I did not hear what they were talking about. After he hung up, my dad asked me to come into the living room. I sat down across from him on the sofa, and he delivered the bad news: Frances had suffocated while taking a bath because she had forgotten to open the window for ventilation. Her funeral would be the following Sunday at Kowloon Union Church.

I don't remember anything about the funeral itself. What I do remember is going shopping the day before at Lane Crawford, Hong Kong's fanciest department store, where I used all my allowance to purchase a small vial of Tea Rose eau de cologne and a Snoopy figurine, things that we had admired together on one of our outings. Even though I knew these items served no practical purpose, I wanted to buy Frances one last present to honor our friendship. I gave the gifts to her mother and said, "Please bury these with Frances."

I have no idea what they did with the gifts, whether they respected my wish or dismissed it as a silly idea from a grief-stricken young friend. That was the last time I saw her parents. They soon moved back to Switzerland to avoid the painful memories of their time in Hong Kong and the loss of their only child. I imagine they must have brought Frances back with them, to be buried in their homeland.

My grandfather is buried at a cemetery on a low mountain ridge southeast of central Taipei, not far from the Taipei Zoo and the Maokong tea plantations. When we visited in the summer of 1978, my mom's side of the family had a small reunion at his tomb with my grandmother and all of their descendants—my mom and her three younger brothers, their spouses and children.

It was the first time I had ever been to a cemetery, but every year after that we repeated the same ritual: a caravan of taxis winding up the steep green hill; a short service of hymns and prayers I did not understand; and countless family photos. We never smiled.

I lived in three countries growing up. Less than three of those years were in Taiwan, yet it's the only place where I've ever spent considerable time in cemeteries and around the rituals of the dead. Even after my parents and I had spent decades living abroad, there was never any question that this was the only ground that mattered.

My grandfather died the same month as Chiang Kai-shek, in April 1975. Chiang had stated that his final wish was to be buried in his native Fenghua in Zhejiang Province, once China and Taiwan were reunified. His wish never came true, and his remains have been kept at a series of temporary mausoleums, most recently at Cihu in Daxi District, awaiting a future that may never come. His son and successor as president of Taiwan, Chiang Ching-kuo, passed away in 1988, and his remains are kept at a different mausoleum in the same area, with the same unfulfilled wish.

Both of their wives outlived them by many years and also died far from home. Soong Mei-ling, better known in the West as Madame Chiang Kai-shek, left Taiwan after the Generalissimo died and emigrated to the United States. She enjoyed a quiet retirement in Upstate New York and lived her final years in an apartment overlooking Central Park, where she passed away in 2003 at the age of 105. By custom she should have had the same resting place as her husband, but she too is in limbo at Ferncliff Cemetery in Westchester, New York. Chiang Fang-liang, the

Chinese name for Faina Vakhreva, was a young Russian worker when she met Chiang Ching-kuo at a machinery plant in Siberia. After marrying Chiang she went with him to China, learned the Ningbo dialect, bore four children, and then followed him to Taiwan where she was the daughter-in-law of the president, and then the first lady. She never again set foot in Russia and died in 2004 at the age of eighty-nine.

Politically, I have no sympathy for the Chiang family. And yet there is an indescribable sadness in being denied that final journey, when the soul is unable to return to its ancestral home.

The first time I experienced Dia de los Muertos was more than a decade ago, when someone invited me to the procession in San Francisco's Mission District. Our mutual friend, Tim, had died in a terrible car accident not long before, and a couple dozen of his friends and coworkers gathered at the parade to share memories, drink beer, and take turns riding an elaborately decorated bike covered with flowers, flashing lights, and smiling photos of Tim whirling around on the wheels. I found the painted skeleton faces; colorful, flouncy attire; abundant candles and marigolds; beautifully decorated altars; and photos of loved ones to be deeply affecting. It never occurred to me that mourning could be so vivid and joyful, that one could focus on remembrance, not just grief.

Years went by, and the losses struck closer to home.

In 2010, I visited Taiwan with my husband and infant son in early January. My brother was supposed to join us from Bangkok, but he called to say he wouldn't be coming because he'd just been diagnosed with liver cancer. He died that September. A month after his funeral, I went to a Halloween party where the hostess and her mother made a Dia de los Muertos ofrenda. They invited me to bring a photo of Ted to add to the altar, a gesture that touched me deeply. Even though my brother had lived for so long in Thailand, he had gone to university in California and was still American to his core. It felt strange to not have a place to visit and remember him in this country.

Four years later, on the evening of July 4, 2014, I flew to Taipei for my mom's funeral. I remember sitting numbly in the airport while the smoke cleared from backyard barbecues and Fourth of July fireworks. The plane left after midnight, propelling me into the twilight zone between darkness and light, between the life I knew and the shadow world, suspended in time and air.

My mom had been sick for so long, but her death still came as a shock. After a period of steady, slow decline, she wound up in the hospital one night with a fever, vomiting, and high blood pressure. Unbeknownst to anyone, she had been suffering from colon cancer, and by the time it was detected, it was stage four and incurable.

After a few days, my mom was allowed to leave the hospital in Sanhsia to go to the bigger hospital in Taipei to get a second opinion. She never made it out of the second hospital. Less than a week after the original diagnosis, she was gone.

My dad had chosen, in advance, the place where he wanted my mom's ashes (and eventually his) to be stored: a columbarium south of Taipei called Tienpin. For a year he kept my mom's ashes in a light pink urn in his living room, and then on the first anniversary of her passing, he arranged for a memorial service at Tienpin.

We were transported there on a chartered minibus, which drove into a mostly unpopulated area of dense trees and vegeta-

tion. We descended down a narrow, steep driveway into a clear-
ing where all the trees had been replaced by a manicured green
lawn. The unusual building was tall and thin with a pointy tower
topped with a cross, and it was decorated with long painted
panels shaped like skis. On the lawn was what appeared to be a
flock of perfectly white sheep, which upon closer inspection we
realized were actually sculptures. It gave the location a pastoral,
peaceful look while subtly advertising its Christian affiliation.
The landscape felt otherworldly, as though some unseen force
had cleared the jungle and placed a mysterious monument there.

After my mom passed away, I returned home to all my usual
routines. I did my best to appear normal, but I was on autopi-
lot, simply going through the motions while struggling with the
enormity of the loss. Even though my mom and I had not lived
in the same country for more than two decades and my memories of her were from another time and place, I was unhinged by
grief. There was no grave to visit here, no church that would say
prayers for her soul, no community of the also-bereaved. Everyone who was close to my mom lived in Taiwan. I came home to
California where no one experienced her absence profoundly,
where no one had to deal with canceling her prescriptions, washing her laundry, throwing away her unopened mail, or staring at
her empty chair.

My grief was overwhelming because there was no context
or container for it. Its free-floating shapelessness terrified me
because that meant it could strike anytime, anywhere, without
warning.

One year later I went back to Tienpin to place my dad's ashes
next to my mom's, and complete the engraving on the plaque
that marked their final resting place. The day of my mom's service, it had been bright and sunny. The day we brought my dad's

ashes to Tienpin, there was a violent thunderstorm. I was happy they were reunited, but my own grief multiplied.

In Chinese folklore, wandering ghosts cause the most trouble. Now I understand it's because they want what we want—to be grounded, to be claimed. Grief works the same way. The more restless it is, the more damage it does. It, too, needs a home.

When I returned to California, I cleared two bookshelves and made an ofrenda with photos of my parents, paper flowers, candles, and objects that held meaning for them—a fountain pen, water buffalo sculpture, origami cranes. Instead of an annual tomb sweeping, I visited the altar daily and kept adding decorations. Slowly I started to feel better.

I don't know when I'll go back to Taiwan. I haven't figured out what will happen to me after I die. My husband and son are in California, but some part of me will always belong to Taiwan. This eternal ache is what it means to live in diaspora. Home, for me, is not an answer but a question.

The Orca and the Spider

On Motherhood, Loss, and Community

1.

Once upon a time, in the Southern Resident community off the coast of the Pacific Northwest, a female orca gave birth to a calf, but the baby died within the hour. The mother, known as Tahlequah, or J35, carried her dead calf for a number of days, attracting worldwide attention in her spectacle of grief. More than a week passed, and Tahlequah showed no signs of letting go, but as she became weaker the other female orcas in her pod took turns carrying the dead calf in a stunning display of maternal support and community.

This was no mere gesture. The calf weighed 400 pounds, and it's estimated that the orca pod swam around 1,000 miles during what came to be known as the "grief tour." Millions of people around the world empathized with Tahlequah and responded by creating essays, poems, and artwork. We are naturally captivated when animals act in ways that seem to fit a human narrative; we instinctively project our own emotions onto other species. Orcas may actually be worthy of the comparison. Among the most intelligent and sensitive of mammals, they travel in organized clans, have complex social interactions, and communicate in a distinct language. Orcas live in matrilineal groups and stay with their mothers their entire lives.

After seventeen days and several waves of news coverage, Tahlequah finally released her calf back into the ocean. The writer Lidia Yuknavitch tweeted:

> Yes, I know I am not this Orca. But her letting go of her dead calf rings through my whole body. Letting my dead daughter go took over a decade—and her life and death became my writing. Sending human mammalian love to an Orca—for what is carried . . .

I, too, was touched by the story and thought about my own experiences with grief. I tweeted in reply:

> I am thinking, our astonishment at the grieving orca reflects a terrible blind spot in our culture. No one who has lost a loved one stops mourning in one news cycle. We carry the grief for longer than anyone ever knows but it is invisible, which only multiplies our pain.

> People are uncomfortable with the orca's spectacle of grief, as though it is abnormal and unhealthy. No. We are the ones who are unhealthy. We expect and push people to get over profound sadness and loss too quickly.

For most people, Tahlequah was a heartwarming story about the power of a community of mothers. For me, it opened up a wound that I didn't yet have the words for.

2.

I grew up in a typical nuclear family: father, mother, sister, brother. We were four sides of a table: a perfect, stable square.

When Ted and I graduated from high school, we always knew we would go to college back in the States, but we didn't really think about what came next. Ted moved to Los Angeles and enrolled at the University of Southern California. By the time I started college at the University of California at Berkeley five years later, he had finished his studies and was back in Hong Kong. Fast-forward a few years: Ted took a vacation in Thailand and liked it so much that he decided to stay. Martial law was lifted, and democracy emerged in Taiwan, making it safe for my parents to return there after nineteen years abroad. I stayed in the Bay Area after graduation. Within a few short years we all dispersed to different countries, separated by borders and oceans, our own miniature diaspora.

From age nineteen onward, I lived on my own in the States with no relatives nearby. I remember sad, solo fast-food meals on Thanksgiving because I was one of the few college students not traveling home for the break. I didn't attend my own graduation ceremony because there was no one coming to watch me walk in my cap and gown. I stressed out whenever I had to fill out an emergency contact form because I did not have someone local who could claim me if I was hurt or in trouble. While these were lonely experiences, I didn't dwell on them or hold any of this against my parents. I simply accepted that we were different from other families, that it was normal to have an ocean between us.

As an adult I visited my parents almost every year and saw my brother every few years. Ted and his partner had three kids, and I eventually married and had one. We settled into a comfortable status quo of periodic visits to Taipei and Bangkok and the easy harmony of grandparents enjoying their golden years with small grandchildren.

Then the health issues started. My brother passed away, and then my mother four years later. My dad never expected to outlive his son and his wife, and his heartbreak hastened his own decline and passing. Within a six-year period, I lost all three of them.

One by one, the sides of our perfect square collapsed. Even though we lived an ocean apart for more than two decades, each loss was like sawing off a table leg, causing the whole structure to wobble and fall. Although my brother and my parents weren't present in my daily life, they provided an invisible scaffolding that I didn't realize I depended on until they were gone. All the things that proved I had a home in California—house, job, passport, driver's license, ability to vote—were the result of choices I had made rather than natural ties to a culture and community. It was a one-sided equation: I could claim it, but it did not claim me. The only true unit of belonging I had that was intrinsic and undeniable and could not be undone, that understood my complicated identity without needing an explanation, was my family.

With each loss, I traveled overseas for the funeral then returned to California where I would be showered with condolences for a week . . . then nothing. There was no grave for me to visit. No fellow mourners to share my loss. No church or temple to advise me on the right rituals. My grief was a secret painfully apparent to me but invisible to others, like a fresh tattoo on unexposed skin. My sorrow was like a stone dropped into a lake that immediately sank to the bottom and made no ripples; like hearing deafening music that no one else could hear. It felt to me like a form of madness, this loneliness that was too profound for words.

3.

The first time I saw *Maman,* one of a series of monumental steel sculptures by the artist Louise Bourgeois, was in Roppongi Hills, Tokyo, where I was on vacation with my husband and son. Since then we've also seen the giant mother spider at the National Gallery of Canada in Ottawa and at the San Francisco Museum of Modern Art. Someone who wasn't familiar with Bourgeois or her work might be surprised at the association of maternal feelings with an insect that usually triggers an instinctive loathing. But a quick look at the descriptive label reveals that Bourgeois appreciates the spiders' industriousness and skill at weaving, a reference to her own mother who was in charge of mending tapestries in the family atelier. She describes spiders as friendly creatures that provide a valuable but thankless service to humans by trapping and eating other insects. Cleaning up, removing obstacles, finding food, and defending the nest: these are all classic examples of a mother's work.

Like mothers, spiders can inspire awe and fear disproportionate to their size. So it's fitting that Bourgeois made the sculptures dramatically oversized, up to nine meters high. Their huge, elongated shadows represent the enormous influence mothers have over their children well into adulthood. Although monstrously large, as if made for a vintage Japanese disaster movie, getting close to *Maman* brings an unexpected feeling of intimacy. You can stand underneath her. You can be enclosed and sheltered by her, the same way your mother once enveloped and surrounded you. The spider mother appears delicate with her fragile skinny legs, but she is literally made of steel.

Maman is stronger than she looks. She is your first and forever home, and she weaves the world into existence.

Native American mythology is filled with tales of a goddess/

ancestor called Spider Grandmother, who weaves the web of creation from which all other living things emerge. Numerous other myths around the world depict spinning and weaving goddesses; the making of textiles was considered a distinctly feminine skill. In her essay "Woven," Lidia Yuknavitch shares a Lithuanian myth about the water spirit Laume, who brings blessings to women who are good weavers and mothers, and judgment to those who are greedy, foolish, or do not protect their children. Weaving, creating, and mothering are intertwined and celebrated as women's work. But the flip side is that being deficient in these arts can lead to violence and punishment.

Every culture has its ways of defining acceptable womanhood.

4.

My own mother did not weave or make clothes, though she did own a sewing machine that she used mostly for hemming and small repairs. But like most mothers, she was a weaver of community, responsible for maintaining the social fabric that cushioned our lives. For decades she had a box with a hinged lid designed to hold index cards for recipes, but she used hers as an address book. It was a bright, sunny yellow with a design of red poppies, and she kept it long after it started to rust at the edges. I still remember my mom's neat handwriting on each lined card and how my own card had been whited out and overwritten numerous times due to my frequent moves. In college I lived in six different apartments over four years; seven, if you count the year I studied abroad in Paris.

My mom's recipe box held addresses and phone numbers for the families we went to church with, my dad's Bible translation colleagues, and others who were part of a large network of Taiwanese Americans on the East Coast and beyond. The box followed our family from place to place; New Jersey in the 1970s, Hong Kong in the 1980s, and then Taiwan in the 1990s, after my parents moved back there for good. I never really thought about the recipe box or what it represented until the 2000s, after my mother was diagnosed with Alzheimer's.

It was around this time that my parents stopped sending Christmas and birthday presents to me in California. Though the gifts were always from the two of them, my mom was the designated gift shopper and the one who kept track of birthdays and special occasions. I received cards and checks for a couple of years, signed in my dad's handwriting, then those stopped too. As my mom slipped further into dementia, it became increasingly difficult for my dad to fill all the gaps.

In retrospect this was a much bigger deal than we were willing to admit. Not because anyone resented the lack of gifts, but because my mom had always been known as an extremely thoughtful and tasteful gift giver, someone who put a lot of effort into beautiful wrapping paper and cards because she took genuine pleasure in it. What hurt was the loss of this part of her personality that we so admired, this form of expression she had lovingly cultivated over a lifetime.

The most refined aspects of her identity were the first to go, followed by the ability to care for others and, ultimately, the ability to care for herself. In between one of my visits to Taiwan and the next, my parents' household spiraled into complete disorder. My mom was no longer capable of basic housework or hygiene, and my dad struggled for months until he hired a housekeeper to help with cooking, shopping, cleaning, and laundry.

In happier, healthier times before the crisis of dementia, my trips to Taiwan had been filled with outings to Taipei for shopping and eating, visits to museums, and sights in the surrounding towns. My parents enjoyed playing tourist with me. We also often visited with relatives on both sides of the family. I saw my dad's family the most because they lived just blocks away from my parents' apartment, and we always made a trip north to Tianmu to see my mom's brothers and their families. It wasn't until near the end of my mom's illness that I realized I hadn't seen any of my mom's family for years, because my dad hadn't thought ahead to make arrangements with them. That's when it really hit me that my mom had been the nucleus at the center of all family gatherings, the planner who brought everyone together.

I didn't notice the unweaving until it was too late. The next time I saw my mom's relatives was at her funeral.

5.

I became a mother myself at the age of thirty-eight. I was lucky that I had a smooth pregnancy with no complications. We hired a doula to hold my hand and coach me through the contractions and pushing. My son arrived at nine o'clock in the morning, and all day long the nurses and staff were in and out of my room, constantly checking on us, until the evening when it became dark and very quiet. While my husband napped on an armchair, my baby and I stared at each other in the moonlight and tried to adjust to this new reality. It was like we were meeting each other for the first time, but also, paradoxically, like we had known each other forever.

My husband's mother came from Canada to stay with us for a month after the baby was born. I was grateful for the help but cautious because my husband's relationship with her was strained. She was volatile and had strong opinions, and I did not want to clash with her over our different approaches to raising a child. The unspoken arrangement was that she would take care of my husband and me, and I would take care of the baby. She managed the shopping, cooking, and cleaning, and she had jurisdiction over the entirety of our apartment except for our bedroom, the inner sanctum where I stayed with the baby and where she only appeared when invited in.

My mother-in-law was a superb cook and she fed and cared for us well, in addition to spoiling her grandson with toys and clothes. I became closer to her over time, and somewhere inside me a door I had forgotten about swung open. But it would not open all the way because what I really wished for and could not have was my own mother by my side. By then my mother was living in a senior care facility in a suburb of Taipei. My dad worked during the week at home, then he commuted two hours north every Friday so he could spend the weekend with her. Neither of them could travel anymore; their last international trip had been to California to attend my wedding four years before. When their grandson was born, they shared their joy and well wishes over the phone.

After my mother-in-law left, we were on our own. Because we didn't have any relatives near us, there were no extra hands when we needed them, no sources of maternal wisdom, no endless supply of hand-me-downs. I learned how to be a mother from my friends and from the internet.

My son is eleven now, and for the most part I think we've done a good job raising him. He visited his Taiwanese grandparents several times and has good memories from before they got sick and passed on. He also spent time with his Canadian grandma but hasn't seen her in several years. For complicated reasons we are no longer in touch with her, and the story behind that particular pain isn't mine to tell.

I envy my friends who have healthy parents that live nearby, who have the ability to slip out for a spontaneous date night or to take off on a weeklong, kid-free vacation. How I wish we had occasional help that we didn't have to pay for—something my friends take for granted—although it was never about the money. How I wish I had a sibling or cousin with children in the same city so that we could send our kids to the same school, share dinners and holidays, coordinate vacation plans, and so on. How I wish my son could grow up with a clan, a group of mothers and children traveling together through life like a pod of orcas, always looking out for each other, secure in their belonging to something bigger than a family of three.

The older he gets, the more I worry that I have not done enough to knit a tapestry that will enfold and protect him, that will open doors and give him room to stretch while keeping him out of harm's way, that will imprint a pattern so deep and recognizable that he can always find his way home. This is what I am most afraid of: that I will be exposed as the mother who cannot weave, who cannot on her own produce the work of many hands, the unseen web that no one notices but everyone needs. Try as I might, there is no material stronger than kinship.

6.

I used to visit Taiwan almost every year. When I was younger, my parents would make a big deal out of taking me around to see all my relatives and there would be many dinners in fancy Chinese restaurants where we'd get a private room and enjoy an elaborate, ten-course feast. No two meals were the same, although I came to understand there would always be a whole fish and a soup course at the end. The occasion for the gathering would be "Gu-lace-uh tńg-lâi" (Grace has come home) and I was always amused by the formality of it, as if my aunts and uncles thought each visit might be my last.

When my parents were still healthy, we were constantly invited to social gatherings—lunch at an oolong tea plantation, day trips to see artisan pottery in Yingge or the Ju Ming sculpture garden, outings to the golf club where my cousin is a member. There was never any shortage of things to do or people to see. But once my dad's health started to decline, my trips were less about sightseeing and more about going to the hospital and navigating a bureaucracy that was totally unfamiliar to me. There were many things expected of me as my parents' daughter, and my cousins took turns chaperoning me to renew my Taiwanese passport, enroll in national health insurance, pay hospital and hospice bills, visit a notary to draw up a will, pay property taxes on my dad's apartment, open a bank account to handle funeral and estate expenses, and so on. I was not consulted on any of these things but simply showed up when I was told to, brought my Taiwanese ID card, and got used to signing my name in Chinese characters. I let my cousins do all the talking for me, understanding nothing except the obligatory backstory when they explained to each new clerk that I was the one who grew up in America and forgot how to speak Taiwanese along the way.

Only when I returned to California did I appreciate the power of this network in Taiwan and the fact that it sprang up unbidden to meet my needs, already knowing what to do and where I needed help, without me ever having to ask.

Once when I visited Taiwan more than a decade ago—before my son was born, before my dad got sick—I woke up with intense abdominal and back pain triggered by an ovarian cyst and possibly a urinary tract infection. I felt alternately chilled and feverish. My dad called my cousin Un-liang, an ob-gyn, and she recommended going straight to a specific lab to get a blood test and urine test. My aunt and other cousin picked us up in a taxi, and the four of us went to the lab together.

I did the urine sample first then sat down to have my blood drawn. I held a cotton ball over the inside of my arm while we waited for the lab results, then suddenly I felt very nauseous. I stood up to go to the restroom and immediately felt light-headed and closed my eyes. I felt myself sweating and hyperventilating as the blood drained from my head. I began to collapse, but there were people on either side of me holding my arms—my dad and my aunt, and the lab technician and doctor—and when I started to fall they slowly lowered me to the ground, where I laid for several minutes. I remember how cool the floor felt. A thin tube was inserted into both of my nostrils, followed by the command to "Breathe!" I inhaled the oxygen weakly at first, then more steadily.

My body melted into the floor. It felt good, peaceful, the way you are supposed to feel at the end of an intense yoga session when lying in savasana, dead body pose. I had the contradictory sensations of feeling light as air, almost high, yet firmly rooted to the ground. I heard the murmur of voices but didn't understand what was being said. Once the nausea passed and my breathing returned to normal, I had a strange sense of well-being; a profound sensation of letting go and being held as I fainted, of being slightly outside my body as though observing my pain instead of living through it. But I never lost consciousness—on the contrary, as my body went limp, my perceptions intensified. The feeling of complete and utter vulnerability took me by surprise because I had not expected it to be so beautiful.

7.

More than a year ago I began to feel an acute and specific fatigue. I was spending a lot of time doing and organizing things for other people, but my labor felt invisible. I took charge of group projects. I planned outings and dinners. I bought more books than I could possibly read, attended nonstop literary events, and cheered for my friends' successes, all while working at a demanding full-time job. I did all of these things willingly, until I reached a point where I felt completely hollowed out. I was putting so much energy into my community, and it felt like it wasn't being reciprocated.

Although I was desperate to exhale and unwind, I was afraid that if I pulled back, the things I cared about wouldn't happen, or worse, I would be left out and life would go on as usual. My absence would not leave a hole in anyone else's Thanksgiving or birthday or baby shower. Everyone else was already secure in their own community with their own built-in schedule of rituals and celebrations. Even though I have excellent friendships, I still felt as though I was on the margins, so my subconscious reaction was to try to move closer to the center by being the one who organized things. The only way I could guarantee myself an invitation to the party, I reasoned, was if I planned the party myself.

My exhaustion carried on for weeks. I could barely drag myself to the grocery store or cook anything that required more than two steps. My husband did more than his share at home, but even then, I struggled to summon the energy to do the few things required of me. The thought constantly spinning in the back of my head was, *Can someone else do this? Does it have to be me?* I fantasized about having a sister nearby, on whose sofa I could collapse and who would happily feed my family if I was too depleted. I thought about how much more time I'd have for myself if I wasn't always the one who had to drive my son to and from every guitar lesson and basketball practice and play date. I dreamed of how nice it would be not to have to pay for ten weeks of summer camp, because as a working parent with no family nearby, I had no other choice.

It seemed like everyone else had a support system to help them, that they could count on without even asking. For a while I withdrew from my social life and felt hurt and resentful, until I finally realized that it wasn't my friends who were letting me down. It was not their fault. What was causing my depletion was the absence of a familial support system, an unforeseen consequence of my family history and the forces of diaspora that separated me from my relatives and landed me in a country where I was comfortable with the language and culture but had no network to sustain me. Where I had to do everything myself.

8.

Distributed computing is the model that gave us the internet. When multiple computers are networked together, they can process much larger computational loads than they can handle individually. The effort is shared among all the member computers; the more members there are, the stronger the network and the greater its overall capacity.

All social media is built on this foundation, with the goal of connecting more people and broadening the network. It mimics the way we build communities, but it is not a substitute for the community, even though the tech companies would like you to think they are synonymous.

Just as larger networks are more powerful and resilient, smaller networks are less capable and more fragile. Every gap is a threat, every hole has the potential to grow bigger, to loosen and unravel the web. A true community, like a tapestry, is both the structure and the story. It provides both form and meaning, and one can't exist without the other. An online social network, while beneficial, can only go so far. I can't call my Facebook friends to pick up my son from school if I'm going to be late. I can't expect my Twitter friends to bring dinner over if I'm feeling burned out and unable to take care of anyone.

And so I come back to the orca and her lesson for me: I can't bear the weight of my sadness alone. I need a pod to lessen the load, to help me carry what I can't carry myself. There's a Vietnamese expression of condolence that captures this feeling perfectly: "chia buồn" translates as "dividing sadness" or "sharing your sadness" to convey that you don't need to bear your burdens alone.

From the spider mother I've learned that weaving a strong network is the key to survival. The electronic kind is good for connecting people, but it's not a substitute for physical presence, for the hands and feet and backs that can actually lighten your load. Apart from giving birth, building the network is the most important women's work and the most significant act of creation that makes everything else possible.

A Book from the Sky

I vividly remember the first time I saw *Tianshu* (*Book from the Sky*) by the Chinese artist Xu Bing. It was at the Inside Out: New Chinese Art exhibition co-presented by the Asia Society and the San Francisco Museum of Modern Art in 1999. Unlike the works by a few other artists that were easily accessible to an American audience, *Tianshu,* by contrast, struck me as more subtle, drawing on a deep knowledge of Chinese history and language. As a Taiwanese American living in the diaspora with very minimal Chinese language skills, the work had a profound effect on me.

Tianshu is an installation that fills an entire room. It consists of dozens of copies of a book arranged in a grid on the floor, each open to a different page, along with massive hanging scrolls of the same text suspended from the ceiling and giant wall panels. Each book is printed and hand-stitched with blue cloth covers in the style of a Song or Ming Dynasty manuscript. The monumental size of the installation is awe inspiring and lends *Tianshu* a palpable authority, as though we are looking at ancient sutras containing timeless wisdom. But here's the catch: the books and scrolls are inscribed with 4,000 made-up Chinese characters painstakingly hand-carved by the artist. Each word has real components of Chinese language, recombined in ways that follow the rules of writing but lack any actual meaning. The symbols represent form without content: they are literally illegible.

The work was first exhibited at Beijing's National Art Museum of China in 1988, where it provoked a range of reactions. Many admired the work's fine craftsmanship while others appreciated its calculated absurdity. Some searched in vain for at least one intelligible character and left angry, insulted by the inaccessibility of the text. Before long, the government condemned the work and shut down the exhibition, judging it to be subversive and mocking centuries of Chinese culture with art that appeared classical (referencing established traditions of bookbinding and calligraphy) but was actually meaningless.

For me, *Tianshu* had a very deep meaning; it replicated the feeling of being locked out of Chinese and Taiwanese culture due to the language barrier and having access only to superficial forms of belonging. Living in New Jersey in the 1970s, my parents wanted me to assimilate; when I stopped speaking Taiwanese upon entering preschool, they didn't fret. In high school, I studied Mandarin for a couple of years and learned to write some characters, but I didn't keep up with it. My abilities in both languages remain very basic to this day.

Tianshu evoked for me a familiar feeling of loss—of something missing, of a flaw that spoils the whole. The work affirmed my diasporic position of standing outside and looking in, of being denied access to something that was familiar but just out of reach. It challenged what had always felt to me like a binary definition of identity: either you are Taiwanese or you are not, with language being the litmus test I would never pass. *Tianshu* opened up the possibility of a third space for someone like me who was neither an insider nor a foreigner, but in between.

In the Western imagination, China seems like a monolith—a vast country and culture that's opaque and unknowable, protected both literally and symbolically by a great wall. There are no shortcuts in learning about it, not even a shared alphabet. It takes years for a non-native speaker to develop functional literacy in Chinese. Xu plays with this sense of enormity in *Tianshu*, both in the size of the installation as well as the time-consuming labor of designing and carving 4,000 distinct characters one at a time. *What would motivate Xu to take on the daunting task of creating his own language completely by hand?* I wondered.

Born in Chongqing in 1955, Xu lived through the cataclysm of Mao's Cultural Revolution from 1966 to 1976. The son of a history professor and a librarian who both worked at Beijing University, Xu experienced firsthand the persecution of families that were considered elitist by the Maoist government. Traditional sources of knowledge such as literature and antiquities were deemed "bourgeois" and destroyed, replaced by the orthodoxy of Mao's *Little Red Book.* Seeing how words could be weaponized to justify political purges made Xu question the reliability of language. Xu also grew up during the government's campaign to replace classical Chinese with simplified characters, resulting in two competing systems for writing. Although Xu has resisted giving an official interpretation of *Tianshu,* one can see how these events could make him view language as slippery and untrustworthy and strive for a new form of artistic expression without historical baggage.

The title of the work bears additional personal significance for me. The character "tian" (天) can mean sky, heaven, or god. *Tianshu,* therefore, can also be translated as a "divine book" or "book from the gods." Although Gutenberg is often credited for inventing the printing press, publishing the first mass-printed Bibles, the Chinese invented movable type 400 years earlier, around 1040 CE. My father carries both these lineages. As the first Taiwanese person to receive a PhD in biblical studies from Princeton Theological Seminary, he went on to have a life-long career in Bible translation and a role in setting up a Bible printing press in China. He was fluent in at least four languages (Taiwanese, Japanese, Mandarin, and English), with working knowledge of several more, including Hebrew and Greek. Like Xu, he had the ethos of a scholar, marked by a deep and sustained focus on a singular topic over multiple years. In a way, they are kindred spirits.

What *Tianshu* gave me was a sense of relief—it didn't matter that I couldn't read it, because no one could. For once I was in on the joke; I didn't feel judged or inferior, I was equal with everyone else. Like my father, the translator, the work provided an opening for me to be accepted and to belong. In my quest to connect more fully with my culture, *Tianshu* symbolized not a wall but a bridge.

Unfinished Translation

The border between one year and the next slowly unfurls; the first day of the new year wrapping its arms around the globe with Tonga celebrating first, and then moving westward across all the continents, reaching American Samoa last. A crooked seam bisects the Pacific Ocean, separating today from tomorrow.

Long ago, I accepted the fragmentation of time zones and the strangeness of a phone call in which Tuesday can talk to Wednesday. Living in a different country from my parents, the time difference was just another border we crossed without a second thought.

My dad and I were both born in January, thirty-four years apart. January is named for Janus, the Roman god of time, beginnings, endings, and transitions; of passages, doorways, and gates. His two faces represent duality, looking in opposite directions toward the past and future. According to Western astrology, we're Capricorns—pragmatic, serious, deskbound. You can count on us, just like you can count on New Year's Day always being on January 1.

But if you look at the lunar calendar—used by Taiwan and other Asian nations to determine holidays—Lunar New Year is more fluid. It skips around, landing somewhere between late

January and late February. In the lunar calendar, our birthdays are at the end of the year, not the beginning. I am fascinated by the mismatch of these two systems, the fact that we can occupy two temporal spaces simultaneously, existing in a liminal zone that is transitional and transnational, belonging to both and neither. This zone can serve as a bridge, but it can also be a point of misunderstanding.

I asked a friend if there's a name for someone who is born during the overlap of the Western and lunar year. She said that we would be considered the "tail" of our Chinese zodiac sign. Think of a year as an animal that stretches across twelve months. In the Gregorian calendar, January is the head and December is the tail. In the lunar calendar, February is the head and January is the tail.

My dad was born in 1935, the Year of the Pig, but January would be considered the tail of the previous year, the Year of the Dog. I was born in 1969, the Year of the Rooster, but January is the tail of the Year of the Monkey. I wonder if there's a mythological creature that combines these attributes; I try searching online, but the closest I can find is a qilin, an auspicious horned beast with the features of a dragon, ox, and lion. Perhaps a more fitting metaphor would be the ouroboros, an ancient symbol of a snake curled into a loop eating its own tail, the two ends joined in a continuous cycle of beginning and ending, of duality dissolving into unity.

Symbols fill the space where language fails. As the daughter of a translator and a child of diaspora, I'm often at a loss for words, stumbling over the edges and gaps where we switch from one system to another, where we lack a perfect translation or direct equivalent. I would give you an example, but I can't find one I am satisfied with. I am terrified of getting it wrong. I have written and rewritten this paragraph over and over because the hardest thing to write about is what you don't know. How do I explain that living in two cultures is both abundance and loss at the same time? How do I describe the things I miss from another place and time when I don't have words for them?

I wish I could consult my dad on this—he would know what to say. Now that he's gone, I don't know how to write across this divide, how to navigate all that he knew that I'll never know. But I can tell you about who he was.

My dad was a middle child in a large family—the third of six sons, the fifth of ten children of a Presbyterian minister and missionary who traveled for months at a time spreading the gospel to the indigenous tribes of Taiwan. He grew up wearing hand-me-downs and jostling for an extra bite of rice at a crowded dinner table. Once, he told me, my grandpa bought a brick of peanut brittle that he intended to cut into pieces and sell for a profit at the market the next day. The children, unaccustomed to the luxury of sweets but fearful of their dad's wrath, snuck into the kitchen and took turns licking the peanut brittle with eager, furtive tongues, thinking he wouldn't notice as the block became sticky and lost its shape.

Like many of his generation, my dad was fluent in three languages by the time he went to high school. His mother tongue was Taiwanese Hokkien, which originated with immigrants from Fujian province who settled in Taiwan starting in the seventeenth century. When my dad was growing up, Taiwanese was mainly spoken in private with family members at home. Between 1895 and 1945, Taiwan was a colony of Japan, so my dad's second language was Japanese, the official language of business, education, and the media. His schooling up until World War II ended was conducted entirely in Japanese, and he and his siblings called each other by their Japanese nicknames from childhood well into their old age.

The third language he learned was Mandarin, which became the official language after Japan surrendered in World War II and the Republic of China took control of Taiwan. After Chiang Kai-shek and the Kuomintang (Nationalist) army arrived in 1949, Taiwanese Hokkien and indigenous languages were banned by the Kuomintang to consolidate power, and they remained underground for nearly four decades under martial law.

It was not until my dad was in college in the late 1950s that he began to seriously study English. His Christian faith and ability to master the fourth (and most difficult) language distinguished him from his peers and set him on a trajectory that led to graduate school in the United States and a PhD from Princeton Theological Seminary. He would go on to become an expert in Bible translation.

My dad mastered four languages before I was even born. He navigated far beyond what he could have imagined as the impoverished son of an itinerant minister in colonial-era Taiwan, traveling the world to supervise translation projects that took him from Canadian First Nations reservations to the islands of Micronesia and everywhere in between. I wonder if he knew that the great distances he traveled and the struggles he overcame would one day make it harder for his daughter to find her way back.

I once interviewed my dad about his Bible translation work. He said that interpretation was the first step—referring back to and explaining the meaning of the original text (in this case, Greek or Hebrew)—and translation was the second step, explaining into the target language. "What language is the interpretation done in?" I asked him. He said that it would normally be in the target language, but sometimes a third language is needed when the translator doesn't know Greek or Hebrew. The interpretation is produced in a third language, such as English or Chinese, and then translated from the third language into the target language.

Many of the projects my dad oversaw were translations into various indigenous languages in China and Taiwan, and he was often the final editor and arbiter of the translation, checking the drafts against the original Hebrew or Greek. A circular process, ending where it began.

In 1960, when my dad boarded an airplane for the first time, it took twenty-seven hours to fly from Taipei to New York, with refueling stops in Oakland, where I live now, and somewhere in the Pacific, probably Hawaii. Today I can make that same trip nonstop in sixteen hours. Although the miles are the same no matter which direction I fly, the psychic distance is greater when I travel to Taiwan. I lose a day in transit and feel like I can never catch up. The flight duration is identical, but the experience is asymmetrical; my body sags with an unnamed ache when going toward a place where my dad no longer waits for me, where I am still learning to speak for myself.

I tell myself the journey will get easier. If time and words are not fixed in stone, maybe there is a version of my life where I am not too late, a translation that will make me whole. Maybe the language where I live is not the end point but an interval—a rest stop on the way home.

One Day You'll Need This

Dear Son,

I have taken you to Taiwan many times and hope we can go again before too long. But there will come a day when you decide to return on your own, when you aren't just tagging along but are propelled by some inner motivation or curiosity to learn about your heritage and your ancestors. If that should happen when I am no longer around to guide you, I want to leave you these instructions so that you can return to the places that matter.

When I was growing up my parents took me to Taiwan many times, and after they moved back I visited almost every year. They used to pick me up at the airport; from the minute I arrived I never had to worry about getting around on my own. But eventually I had to learn to navigate by myself. None of these addresses are written down; everything I know is from memory and repetition.

You haven't had this lifelong training, and you don't know any Taiwanese or Mandarin, so you will have to travel twice as far to reach the same place. I once felt this way too—like Taiwan was distant and unknowable, a locked box. But one day it will call to you. When you go, bring this letter and these four photos with you.

The Airport

You passed through here when you were only eight months old, on your way to meet Grandma and Grandpa for the first time. You probably don't think of the airport as a place of any significance; I didn't either until the eve of Lunar New Year 2000, when I was denied entry and detained overnight because my US passport had expired. My heart still pounds thinking about it. I was all alone, stranded at an international border, unable to prove my identity, dealing with hostile immigration officials who looked down on me for not speaking the language.

Let my mistake be a lesson to you: always double-check your passport before you go abroad!

Mackay Memorial Hospital

Ever since I was a child, before I knew how to get around Taipei by myself, the hospital with the red brick colonnade on Zhongshan Road has always been part of my mental map, an imaginary midpoint between the shopping district around Taipei Main Station and the Grand Hotel.

This hospital is where I took my first breath and where Grandpa took his last. During Grandpa's final year, I spent countless hours in those forlorn hospital rooms, leaving only to get food or to walk down the hall to call you and Dad. One time an entire family silently gathered at the window at the end of the hallway. I thought they were eavesdropping on us, but then I realized they were just watching the sunset, seeking a moment of relief from their own vigil.

To get there, take the MRT red line and get off at Shuanglien.

You can also get into a cab and say "MA KAI" and they will know you mean here.

Church on Linsen Road

Walking distance from Mackay (MRT: Zhongshan) is Zhongshan Presbyterian Church; my parents always called it "the church on Linsen Road." You can't miss its distinctive Gothic architecture occupying a corner surrounded by high-rises.

We were there in the summer of 2016 for Grandpa's memorial. I was nervous because I was asked to read a short piece of writing for the service. Unlike Grandma's funeral in 2014, I was the only immediate family member left, so all eyes were on me. For the first time ever, I had to represent my family. Hundreds of people attended Grandpa's service, and a few even came from overseas. So many people came up to offer condolences, and even though I couldn't understand them, their sad eyes and gentle hands on my shoulder said everything.

But you know what I remember most? One of Grandpa's friends showed me a narrow corkscrew stairway that led to a small balcony above the nave where they control the lights and audiovisuals. He explained in English that when Grandpa was a young man, he was the choir director at this church, which was how he met Grandma. During breaks in choir practice, the two of them would sneak up to the balcony and Grandpa would share a piece of candy with her secretly, away from everyone else. What an unexpected gift, this memory of sweetness on the saddest day.

If anyone asks who you are, show them the photo of Grandma's big book—the Kao Family History—and tell them you are descended from the same ancestor as Rev. Kao Chun-ming 高俊明.

Yangmingshan

Yangmingshan is a national park at the northern edge of Taipei that's famous for sulfur hot springs and cherry blossoms. It's also where Taiwan Theological Seminary is located and where my family lived when I was born. At the time, Grandpa was the youngest ever dean of the seminary. All my baby photos were taken here.

The seminary is where my parents met the American missionaries who were the reason our family fled to the United States in 1971. Every story I tell comes back to this moment: it's why I grew up American.

Twenty years later, martial law was finally lifted, and Grandma and Grandpa returned permanently to Taiwan. Grandma was hired as a professor at the seminary, and they moved back to Yangmingshan for a few years. The only house my family has ever lived in, we lived in twice.

To get there, take bus 109 from Jiantan MRT Station (near the Shihlin Night Market) or bus 260 from Taipei Main Station. Walk past the main seminary building with the pagoda and look for the house with tan hua, Grandma's favorite flower that blooms once a year.

Sanhsia

"Sanhsia" (also spelled "Sanxia") means "three gorges"—a place where three rivers meet. Grandma and Grandpa lived their final years here in an apartment complex of tall pink towers with a koi pond in the courtyard. Do you remember that apartment we visited so many times—where you watched cartoons, ate platters of cut guava and mango, where you and Grandpa batted around a balloon in the living room before Parkinson's took its toll on him? That home no longer exists except in our memories. But you can still find Great Auntie's family at the compound a few blocks away, the closest thing we have to an ancestral home.

I once had a nightmare that I couldn't remember how to get to Sanhsia, so I wrote it down. Take the MRT yellow line to Jingan Station. When you exit, look for a sign of a man with a thick beard (that's Formosa Chang, a Taiwanese bento chain) to find the bus stop. Take bus 908 to Sanhsia and get off on Zhongshan Road right after you see the temple. Turn right on Ren Ai Road and you'll see a green and white sign for your uncle's dental clinic (by the time you visit it will be run by his son, Johnny). When you arrive, show them the photo of you, me, and Grandpa, and they will erupt with recognition and invite you in.

Tienpin

The final place I want you to visit is the hardest to get to but the most important. You will have to take a taxi; show this to the driver: 天品山莊. Tienpin is the columbarium where Grandma and Grandpa's ashes are kept. Do you remember the twisty roads leading to the vaguely church-shaped building next to a lawn decorated with fake sheep? Inside are endless hallways of pristine white niches, like lockers for the dead. At the lobby, show them the photo of the inscription on Grandma and Grandpa's niche, and they will help you find it.

The niche is at knee level; they will give you a stool and a small key to unlock it. Grandpa is in the green urn and Grandma is in the pink one. Remember when you made that rose out of gold origami paper? I put it in the niche last time I visited. Now it's your turn to add something—the last photo, the one of me.

This will be my reunion with Grandma and Grandpa. Close your eyes and stay for a while. Try to remember their voices, and mine. Hum the tune I taught you, the famous hymn written by Great Grandpa, and you will feel a breeze as the spirits of your ancestors embrace you and welcome you home.

Always with you,
Mom

Acknowledgments

I have so many people to thank for supporting me and my writing over the years. First and always: I owe everything to my AAPI writing group, Seventeen Syllables, who've kept me going for more than two decades (through many waves of despair and uncertainty, and innumerable Lit Crawl readings) and whose feedback, support, and hospitality have nourished me through all the phases of writing *The Translator's Daughter*. Lillian Howan, Caroline Kim, Brian Komei Dempster, Jay Dayrit, and Marianne Villanueva, plus past members Grace Talusan, Roy Kamada, Sabina Chen, Brynn Saito, and Edmond Chow—you all are family to me. Garrett Hongo, arigato for your tough love as our original sensei.

I'm grateful to Hedgebrook's Writer-in-Residence Program and the Ragdale Foundation, who provided early support for my writing and took a chance on me before I'd published anything. Twenty years passed before I could do a residency again; many thanks to Writing Between the Vines for a dreamy week in Sonoma where I revised portions of this book.

Much love to Elmaz Abinader, my professor, advisor, and friend, who helped me believe in my work and show up for myself, over and over again; and shoutout to the Mills College MFA community. Capricorns rule!

Gratitude to Voices of Our Nations Arts Foundation (VONA) for nurturing writers of color before it was a thing; and to Tin House for the best virtual workshop I've ever attended—gracias to Marcelo Hernandez Castillo and my Winter 2021 workshop cohort.

The Writers Grotto has been a great community where I've met so many talented writers who have been generous with advice, time, and friendship, in particular: Maw Shein Win, Vanessa Hua, Rita Chang-Eppig, Faith Adiele, Preeti Vangani, Dominic Lim, Peg Alford Pursell, and Bridget Quinn—thank you! Extra abundant love to Susan Ito, my friend, neighbor, and fellow memoirist, Grotto member, Mills alum, and OSU press mate—everything is better when you're part of it.

To the entire team at Mad Creek Books—sincerest thanks for seeing the value in my work and for shepherding *The Translator's Daughter* to completion, especially Editorial Director Kristen Elias Rowley for your care and thoughtfulness as an editor; Rachel Cochran and Taralee Cyphers for keeping everything on track; Joy Castro, series editor for Machete, for your expansive editorial vision; the design team for creating a beautiful cover; and Samara Rafert for helping to get the word out. Special thanks to independent translator Jenna Tang, who helped with copyediting and provided critical review of my writing about Taiwanese language, history, and culture; and to J. D. Beltran for my author photo.

Deepest appreciation to my literary heroes who were kind enough to provide endorsements for this book: Matthew Salesses, Grace Talusan, Shawna Yang Ryan, Beth Nguyen, Jami Nakamura Lin, and Michelle Kuo. Thank you from the bottom of my heart.

I'm indebted to the editors and lit mags that published my pieces over the last few years and continue to cheer me on:

Nicole Chung, Sari Botton, Christopher James, Jiksun Cheung, Bryan Fry, Vonetta Young, Pat Matsueda, Adam Sternbergh, and others, thank you for championing my work. Portions of this book have previously appeared in *Ninth Letter, Hedgebrook Journal, Cha: An Asian Literary Journal, Washington Square Review, KHÔRA, Blood Orange Review, The Manifest-Station, Memoir Mixtapes, Jellyfish Review, Catapult, Longreads, The Offing, Artsy,* and *The Bureau Dispatch.*

Biggest hugs to my *KHÔRA* family—Kirin Khan, Sagirah Shahid, and Shane Rowlands for your brilliance; Leigh Hopkins, for being the loveliest and most supportive editor; and Lidia Yuknavitch for providing space, support, and encouragement to this sacred, beautiful garden.

Endless thanks to my Memoir Sisters—Jen Soong, Grace Hwang Lynch, and Anne Liu Kellor—for advice, commiseration, and sharing the ups and downs of this journey with me; and to the XLBs for being my Taiwanese American support system— Grace HL, Linda Shiue, Yi Shun Lai, Lisa Chiu, Esther Tseng, and Catherine Chou. Truly, this is the sisterhood I've always wanted.

Priscilla Kalugdan, Chaincy Kuo, Gloria Chen-Rollins, and Philip Krayna: thank you for your sustaining friendship and for believing in me long before I could call myself a writer. Heart emojis to many other friends not listed here and the broader writing community I've met online, who've stuck with me through the rejection trenches and helped celebrate my wins.

Pan Chih-ming, it's unlikely you'll ever see this, but I will never forget your kindness that day at the airport. John G., thank you for coming to my rescue when you didn't have to.

My extended family in Taiwan has been there for me through everything, and even though we can't communicate easily, I hope you know how much I appreciate all of you. There aren't adequate words to express my gratitude to Uncle I-to and Auntie Huichin, who helped me in countless ways when my parents could not; without you I would have floated out to sea. Deepest thanks to Auntie Tōa-ko· and her family for ensuring my dad and mom were never short of care or companionship; as a long-distance daughter, this is a debt I can never repay. Un-chun, thank you for steering me through all the financial and administrative minutiae; I could never have completed this obstacle course without you. Auntie Sī-ko·, you were also a great help to my parents during a time of need. Much love to Aunt Emi for the mahjong games and for keeping me connected to Mom's side of the family; and to Uncle Yoshi for documenting the Kao family history. And finally, much gratitude to my cousin's son 朱怡康, who adopted my dad's dog, Teddy, and has given him the best life. Every time I see a picture of Teddy, I'm reminded of my dad's love.

To my American cousins Leng (and Lisa), Ben, Ken, Emily, and David—thanks for "getting" me; your moral support matters more than you know. Diana, Lainey, and Keith: your hospitality over the years helped us feel less alone. To Ted's wife—you are my sister, always.

Anil, words aren't enough to convey how much I appreciate you and the endless ways you have supported me during the writing of this book and as my lifelong partner. As a fellow writer, I'm grateful that you understand the sacrifices that go into making art. I love you.

Eternal cuddles and boops to Mimi (RIP) and Amber for being there for me.

Mom, Dad, and Ted, I'm sad you won't be able to read this book, but I think you've always known this was for you. I'd like to imagine the three of you all playing a competitive game of Scrabble in the afterlife. I miss you every day, and I hope you are proud of me.

To the next generation—Jenny, Shelly, and Billy, and to Devin most of all—please look after yourselves and know that wherever life takes you, you will always have a place in Taiwan. Don't wait too long to go back.

Machete

Joy Castro and Rachel Cochran, Series Editors

This series showcases fresh stories, innovative forms, and books that break new aesthetic ground in nonfiction—memoir, personal and lyric essay, literary journalism, cultural meditations, short shorts, hybrid essays, graphic pieces, and more—from authors whose writing has historically been marginalized, ignored, and passed over. The series is explicitly interested in not only ethnic and racial diversity, but also gender and sexual diversity, neurodiversity, physical diversity, religious diversity, cultural diversity, and diversity in all of its manifestations. The machete enables path-clearing; it hacks new trails and carves out new directions. The Machete series celebrates and shepherds unique new voices into publication, providing a platform for writers whose work intervenes in dangerous ways.